1000

1000

DREAMS

· INTERPRETED ·

Michael Powell

BARRON'S

Contents

Introduction

Dreams are fascinating and bewitching. They reflect our deepest desires and our greatest fears; they remind us of our goals and the obstacles we must overcome to reach them; some even believe they provide a tantalizing glimpse into the future.

What do the symbols that appear in our dreamscape mean?

How can they help us to interpret our lives and gain access to

our untapped resources? This book provides a thousand practical

explanations to help the reader unlock these secrets and is a

compelling introduction to the hidden language of dreams.

People and
Places

1 heart

Dreaming of your heart, the emotional hub of your being, indicates that there is an imbalance in some part of your personal life that is blocking love.

2 nose

To dream about your nose signifies that you are pursuing your goals with single-minded determination; if your nose is bleeding, make sure you are not harming yourself or anyone else to reach them.

3 beard

A beard represents virility, but it may also be inviting you to take a more flexible approach to your emotions and to assert individuality over certain cultural norms.

4 long hair

Dreaming of long hair symbolizes your fear of growing old and may also warn of a corresponding trouble in business and the need to determine your real priorities.

5 moustache

A moustache stands for intrigue and political posturing; now is the time to gather trusted allies as a busy period enters its final phase.

6 belly

To see a large female belly denotes fecundity and fruitfulness; a large male paunch represents repressed anger and complicated business dealings.

7 brain

Dreaming of your brain suggests a mental upheaval; you may also be neglecting your powers of reason in favor of emotional outbursts.

8 ears

Suppose ears play an important part in your dream; they suggest your willingness to listen to those around you, but they may also represent the need for quiet contemplation.

9 skin

To dream of your skin signifies a preoccupation with your own safety or well-being; if your skin is bleeding, your concerns are probably well founded.

10   face

To see your own face distorted in some way suggests that you are resisting positive change because of a lack of confidence in your own abilities.

11   mouth

Seeing a mouth in your dream is a sign that you are leaving something important unsaid; alternatively, it could be a call for greater discretion.

12   back

To see your own back signifies that others have a perspective on a situation that you cannot see; welcome the advice of others to solve a difficult problem.

13 arms

Arms suggest the interplay between your nurturing instincts and the need to exert dominance in a relationship. Injured arms signify your inability to reach out to give or receive help.

14 breasts

Breasts express a need to give or receive tender nourishment; conversely they may also be encouraging you to move outside your comfort zone.

15 nails

Clean fingernails denote self-respect and good opinion; dirty or broken fingernails suggest disgrace or avoidance of your responsibilities.

16 eyelashes

When your eyelashes grow, a romantic relationship may be about to enter a new and positive phase.

17 entrails

To dream of human entrails indicates that you are harboring guilty feelings that cannot be contained for much longer.

A dream involving injury to your fingers signifies fear of failure with regard to an intricate problem and the need to remain focused on the task at hand rather than anticipated rewards.

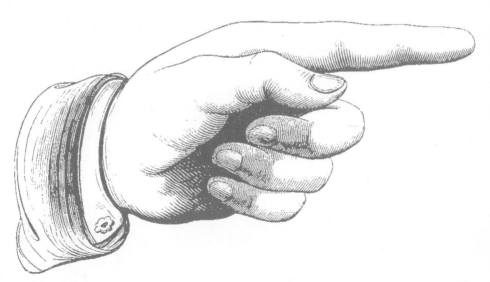

To dream that you have very large hands is a sign that success is within your grasp; it also shows that you are honest in your dealings with others.

20 legs

Dreaming of legs is a call to action; if you admire someone else's legs, then you risk allowing someone else's achievements or opinions to cloud your judgment.

21 lips

Lips signify romance and sensuality; sore lips invite you to take a more light-hearted approach to matters of the heart.

22 muscles

To see muscles in your dream suggests power; to admire your own muscles represents a tendency to solve problems with brawn rather than brain.

23 nudity

To hide your nudity indicates that you are feeling guilty about something that goes against your principles.

24 blood

To dream of blood flowing from a wound denotes bad business dealings; if you see blood on your hands, take care, because bad luck may be just around the corner.

25 liver

To dream of a liver indicates that it is time to distance yourself from people who exert a negative influence or are overly critical of others.

26 skeleton

If you dream that you are a skeleton, you may be eating yourself up with worry; try to relax and be honest about your own needs and feelings.

27 hairy hands

If your hands are covered in hair, you may be hiding the truth to gain advancement; honesty is always the best policy.

28 veins

Dreaming of your veins or arteries corresponds to a positive life-affirming challenge; when something comes easily, beware of taking it for granted.

29 twins

Twins in your dream
correspond to aspects of your
personality that must be
reconciled before you form a
union with like-minded people.

30 crying baby

A crying baby may be a sign that you feel
overlooked and undervalued or that your
creative abilities are being neglected.

31 birthmark

If you dream of a birthmark,
you will be distinguished by your acts.

32 body

Suppose any part of your body is growing out of control. This is a powerful warning that things are running away with you; take a short break to listen to your body's needs.

33 hiccups

If you have hiccups in your dream, it means that someone is thinking of you; a secret admirer may be arranging a meeting.

34 breathing

Difficulty breathing expresses a need to escape from a stressful situation that is damaging your well-being.

35 sneezing

Sneezing expresses your ambivalence about an emotionally charged predicament; repeated sneezing signifies indecision or apathy.

36 inhaling

To dream of inhaling a beautiful scent foretells that your most cherished desires will soon reach fulfillment.

37   toes

To dream of toes corresponds to your sense of balance in life; if your toes are injured or changed in some way, an imbalance that urgently needs addressing may exist.

38   neck

Dreaming about your neck suggests insecurity about a romantic relationship; washing your neck implies a need for a frank appraisal of a long-standing union.

39   body

To lose a part of your body in a dream denotes the loss or letting go of something in your waking life associated with it.

40 speaking

Difficulty in speaking or lacking the power of speech indicates reticence or the inability to get your point across. Or it may warn of false friendships.

41 stammering

Stammering in a dream represents difficulty expressing your needs to those around you; you may also feel that your opinion has been overlooked.

42 ugly

To dream that you are, or have become, ugly encourages you to turn your attention to others rather than dwell on your perceived inadequacies.

43 attractiveness

To dream that you are very attractive hints at areas of dissatisfaction in a close relationship. Are you being honest about your needs?

44 being ill

To be ill in a dream can be a good sign; it may be a warning that something that is going wrong is well within your power to correct.

45 bones

To dream about your bones implies that you are concerned about either your health or your wealth; if your bones are visible, then you are stretching yourself too thin.

46 teeth

To clean your teeth in a dream foretells that diligence and perseverance will be required to conclude a health or financial issue.

47 tongue

To dream of your own tongue relates to your reputation and your linguistic accomplishments; an oral agreement may be causing anxiety.

Wearing feathers on your clothes suggests that you feel able to bear a challenge lightly and with a sense of humor.

49 dirty shoes

If you have dirty shoes, take care to think before you speak or your bluntness may cause offense; new shoes mean positive change and travel adventures.

50 socks

Putting on or removing socks expresses a need for more passion in your relationship; mending a sock represents a compromise in your personal life.

51 slippers

Wearing slippers indicates that you are comfortable in your domestic life, but this may be at the expense of more worldly commitments.

52 backpack

A backpack appearing in your dream indicates your desire to explore new things; emptying a backpack suggests you are seeking the comforts of home.

If you dream of wearing a helmet, you feel mistrustful of someone whom you suspect may be deceiving you.

If you are wearing new gloves, you are circumspect in your dealings with others; old gloves may warn of betrayal. But if you find a pair, your love life will soon blossom.

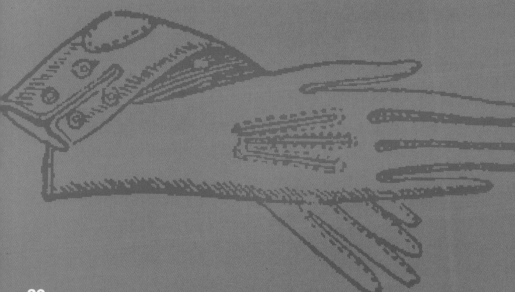

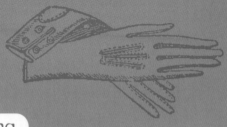

55 yellow clothing

When yellow clothing features in your dream, you can look forward to celebrations and financial benefits; it's time to have some fun.

56 belt

When a belt appears in a dream, it represents a conflict between your desire to be independent and your need for security and support.

57 ill fitting clothes

Dreaming of clothes that are ill fitting suggests that you have taken on a role that is currently making you feel trapped or overwhelmed; but time and familiarity will improve the situation.

58 pajamas

If you are wearing pajamas or nightclothes, you are feeling emotionally vulnerable and are concerned about making a fool of yourself.

59 wearing clothes inside out

To wear your clothes inside out signifies a lack of concern for convention, which may benefit you so long as it is not taken to an extreme.

60 furs

Wearing furs denotes great wealth acquired at the expense of others. Are you conducting your business affairs as fairly as you should?

61 torn clothes

If your clothes are tattered or torn, then you may be feeling insecure about your material possessions and your status among your peers.

62 loose clothing

The wearing of loose clothing expresses a desire to hide your true nature; tight clothes express feelings of being restricted or controlled.

63 umbrella

Seeing or using an umbrella in your dream suggests that you will manage to weather a storm; it is also a reminder that preparation is better than prevention.

64 ribbons

If you are wearing ribbons or other bright decorations, you can look forward to a joyful reunion or an unexpected celebration.

65 necklace

Wearing a necklace may denote a loss, but it also bodes well for the building of new relationships.

66 pearls

Wearing pearls expresses your wish for purity and your interest in spiritual development.

67 jewelry

To lose an item of jewelry warns of betrayal by a close friend; finding or receiving jewelry as a gift brings good luck and romantic adventures.

68 unusual dressing

Wearing clothes you customarily would not wear indicates that you are suppressing important aspects of your personality; your insecurity may be holding you back in social situations.

69 tattoo

To dream of a tattoo indicates that others are judging you superficially; trust in your abilities and you will soon overcome unfounded criticism.

70 robe

Wearing a robe or a cape represents your desire for power or praise; an uncomfortable robe is a sign that your ambition is preventing you from appreciating your achievements.

apron

To dream of wearing an apron implies domestic bliss; if the apron is torn or dirty, then assess whether you feel comfortable in the roles that you have adopted at home and at work.

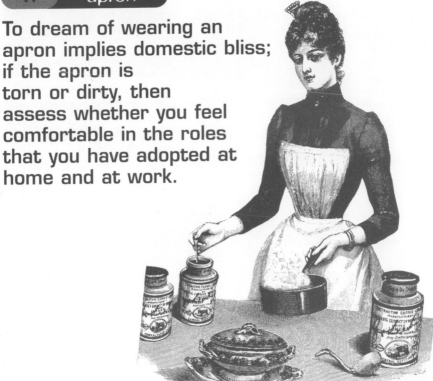

72 stockings

A run in your stocking refers to an inopportune financial arrangement resulting from a hasty or overcautious decision.

73 undergarments

Dreaming of undergarments prompts you to consider whether the image you choose to present to the world is a benefit or a hindrance.

74 sandals

Wearing sandals in a dream represents self-awareness and introspection; it may also be a sign that a spiritual journey is causing conflict with family and friends.

Losing a button alerts you to the possibility that friends or colleagues may not be pulling their weight, leaving you to pick up the pieces.

76 tie

Wearing a tie in your dream may be a sign that you are seeking comfort in established norms or traditions; removing a tie suggests advancement in business.

77 hat

Losing a hat implies that your business dealings may suffer a temporary setback; wearing a new hat signifies a return to traditional methods after a period of change.

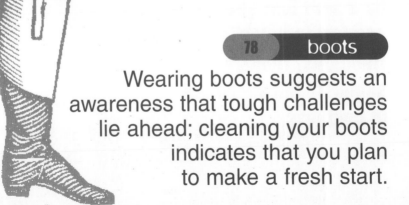

78 boots

Wearing boots suggests an awareness that tough challenges lie ahead; cleaning your boots indicates that you plan to make a fresh start.

Leather appears in your dream to ward off bad feeling and ill will; it brings good luck in business and creates new challenges.

80 mask

A dream in which you are wearing a mask implies your unwillingness to reveal your vulnerability in a relationship; removing a mask indicates self-knowledge about a weakness or mistake.

81 T-shirt

Wearing a plain T-shirt in a dream indicates honesty in your relationships; if the T-shirt bears a slogan or picture, beware of losing your individuality in a group context.

82 veil

Wearing a veil in your dream suggests a lack of honesty with your partner. Are you hiding your true feelings?

83 lipstick

Lipstick is connected to your sexuality and self-image; applying or wearing lipstick highlights an ability to anticipate a future romantic development.

84 hood

Wearing a hood in your dream has symbolic relevance as an expression of spiritual energy but also bears an aspect of concealment; you may be hiding your spirituality or concealing your beliefs.

Wearing a uniform in your dream symbolizes a lack of power in your life or a misplaced sense of direction.

86 doctor

Dreaming of a doctor denotes good health and prosperity; it also indicates a victorious engagement in business or love.

87 firefighter

If you dream of a firefighter make sure you're not chasing risks for the sake of other people's admiration.

88 police officer

If you dream you are the police officer, it may mean that feelings of powerlessness are causing you to retreat into unhelpful fantasies.

89 dentist

To visit the dentist in your dream indicates that you should test the reactions of others concerning a difficult undertaking.

90 religious person

If a priest or rabbi appears in your dream, it may represent your desire for ritual cleansing.

91 soldier

Dreaming of a soldier suggests that a situation may reach an unexpected or disappointing conclusion.

92 landlord

A landlord is a symbol of dominance in your domestic environment; you should examine the way in which power is expressed in your household.

To see a beggar in your dream invites you to examine the motives behind a recent generous act; your magnanimity may be hiding feelings of fear or pride.

94 judge

A judge in your dream highlights your need for dispassionate and objective judgment about a personal crisis.

95 lawyer

To dream of a lawyer is symbolic of gaining advantage in a dispute; try to offer advice and assistance rather than finding fault.

96   balcony

Dreaming of being on a balcony is a reminder that it is not sufficient to see your goals clearly; you must also move toward them.

97   hospital

A dream that takes place in a hospital suggests that you are preoccupied with your health, and may be using it as an excuse to play safe.

98   kitchen

If your dream takes place in a kitchen, it demonstrates your willingness to confront important domestic issues and to look at your alternatives with creativity.

To see or enter a place of worship in your dream invites you to examine the role of spirituality in your life; pay special attention to the people you meet there.

A corridor or alleyway represents feelings of entrapment, but also the security of a chosen path versus the uncertainty of a calculated risk.

101 building

A building or house represents how you see yourself, or how you think others see you; take careful note of its appearance and condition, and the atmosphere inside.

102 hotel

Being a guest in a hotel or someone's house expresses your need for nurture and rest; being an unwanted guest shows that obstacles are preventing you from finding comfort.

103 school

Being in a school or classroom indicates your need to learn new skills in order to advance.

104 cemetery

To see a cemetery signifies an unresolved sense of loss or worries about death; but it can also suggest an anticipated change.

105 crossroads

Encountering crossroads in your dream inevitably corresponds to making a decision; remember that standing still and turning back are both choices.

106 castle

A castle can be a symbol of power and the rewards of your achievements but also of vulnerability and isolation; examine the ways in which you stand to gain and lose security in your waking life.

To see an airport in your dream corresponds to your attitude toward change; it may also refer to a situation from which you seek to escape.

108   island

Seeing an island in your dream signifies comfort after much difficulty; being stranded on an island represents your need for solitude or a wish to escape responsibilities.

109   beach

Dreaming of a beach is often linked with a period of emotional change. New feelings are surfacing and old experiences and memories can be washed away.

110 underground

Being underground expresses a need for greater security and peace of mind; it can also refer to issues that you have buried in the back of your mind.

111 playground

If you find yourself in a playground or amusement park, you should approach a troubling situation in a more playful or relaxed frame of mind.

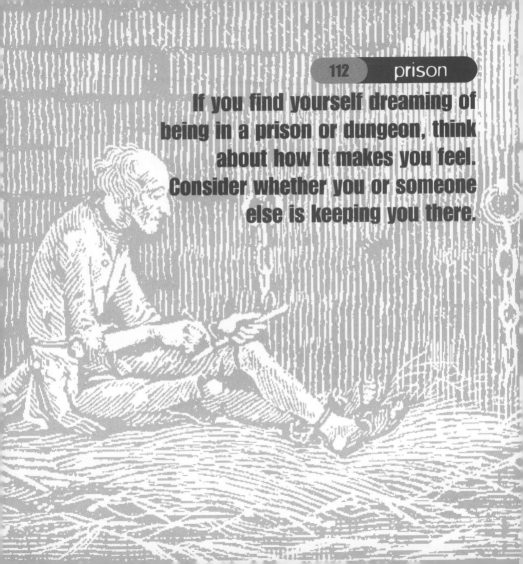

If you find yourself dreaming of being in a prison or dungeon, think about how it makes you feel. Consider whether you or someone else is keeping you there.

113 bookshop

Entering a bookshop in a dream corresponds to your desire for self-improvement and for maintaining a clear mind.

114 bank

To dream of visiting a bank points to your finding a balance between surplus and need; measure what is desirable against what is necessary.

115 sporting goods store

If you find yourself in a sporting goods store, you can take a calculated risk when backed into a corner if you plan carefully.

116 bar

If your dream takes place in a bar, it is a warning that emotions will run high after careless thoughts are expressed; behave with dignity while others lose theirs.

117 hairdresser

If your dream takes place at a hairdresser's, you will enjoy the hospitality of a glamorous and alluring host; do not attempt to outshine your benefactor.

118 train station

A railway station is a busy and sometimes bewildering setting for a dream; it reveals the need to allow the future to take shape without your interference in a restless or impatient manner.

119 waiting room

Finding yourself in a waiting room is linked to your ability to look at developments that may from a distance appear intimidating, without fooling yourself with glib platitudes.

120 theater

A theater or stage is a common location for a dream; it alludes to the relationship between being a spectator and an actor in your waking life.

Crossing a bridge implies traveling over a potential hazard while remaining safely above it; this journey or transition can be completed without confrontation.

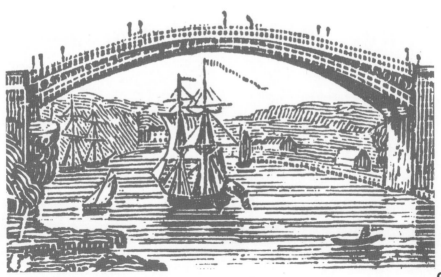

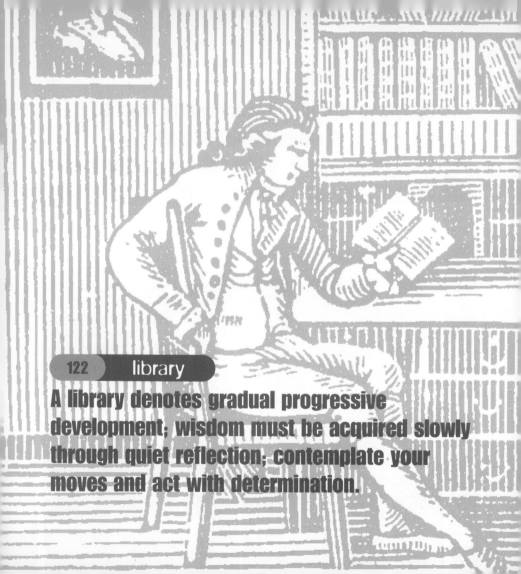

122 library

A library denotes gradual progressive development; wisdom must be acquired slowly through quiet reflection; contemplate your moves and act with determination.

123 lighthouse

To dream of a lighthouse denotes the need for modesty in a high position; consistency of purpose will reassure others that you merit your position.

124 museum

A museum represents a transition from the old to the new; everything in your life may seem to be going smoothly, but pay close attention to a project that is undergoing great change.

Visiting a racetrack in your dream denotes exhilarating uncertainty; you will profit in business by taking an enjoyable risk.

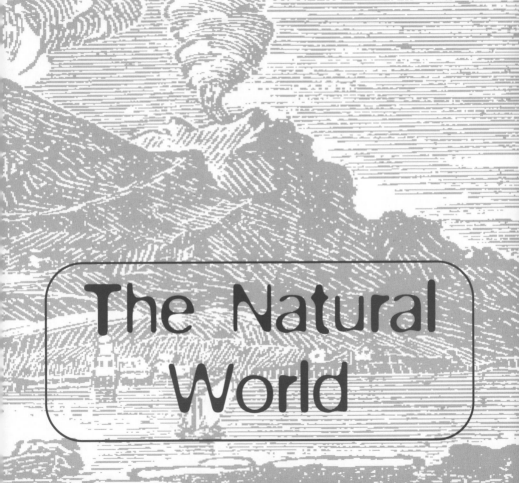

The Natural World

moss

If you dream of moss, you are being reminded of something that you have left undone; it is an invitation to face up to your responsibilities.

127 flint

Flint is a powerful symbol of latent potential; it also alludes to breaking open the heart to encourage spiritual development.

128 quarry

A quarry suggests that a situation in which you previously felt safe now makes you feel susceptible or exposed.

Dreaming of small stones and pebbles suggests that you are troubled by minor worries and are preoccupied with irritating details.

130 rocks

Dreaming of rocks denotes that you will face adversity leading to much unhappiness; if the rocks are wet, you should seek an alternative route.

131 slate

Composed of many compacted layers, slate signifies strength through cumulative, small actions.

132 silver

A dream involving silver is a warning to curb your spending; it may indicate over-reliance on a source of income that you should not take for granted.

133 gold

When gold appears in a dream, you will enjoy unprecedented success in all your endeavors. If you lose gold, then an oversight will cause you to miss a significant opportunity.

134 copper

A dream involving copper may mean that your superiors are causing you anxiety; if the copper is tarnished, it may indicate that you will triumph by impressing those around you.

135 iron

A dream involving iron refers to typically masculine energies; strength without flexibility will take you only part of the way toward your goal.

136 coal

To dream of coal represents dormant energies and bleak unhappiness; if the coal is lit, you will experience transformation and fortunate dealings in business.

137 seeds

To dream that you are sowing seeds indicates that your future plans will bear fruit; harvest time also points to pleasure and plenty.

138 hedge

If you walk beside a green hedge with someone you admire, you should probably open your heart; if the hedge is bare, then you may be fooling yourself about the other person's feelings or even your own.

139 pond

A pond or lake in your dream is a symbol of your receptiveness; it also corresponds to your feminine nature and to a period of calm reflection.

Dreaming of dry sand running through your fingers indicates loss; if you succeed in collecting the sand in your palms, remember that you are still in a desert. It may be time to cut your losses.

Walking against a brisk wind indicates that you are pursuing your goals with determination and courage; if you are being blown along, then it is time to reexamine your priorities.

142 rainbow

If you see a rainbow, something unusual will surprise you; if you are weathering a tough storm, remember that hardship often leads to positive change.

143 snowstorm

A snowstorm is an indicator of unhappiness or disappointment; if you eat snow, you will not fulfill your potential. If the sun shines as it snows you will overcome your adverse fortune.

144 drought

To dream of a drought signifies that much effort is required to resurrect a project or relationship that is lying dormant or neglected

To dream of weather indicates a change in fortunes; to discuss the weather expresses a need to keep others at a polite distance.

146   clouds

When clouds appear, notice their shape and structure. If the clouds are dark and heavy, they express misery and trouble; if the clouds are white, your outlook will improve.

147   mist

To encounter mist or fog indicates a feeling of uncertainty; if the mist is quite heavy, then your hesitancy may be damaging your well-being.

148 shower

A shower of rain on a sunny day denotes youthful energy and lightness of being. Seeking shelter from it represents a withdrawal from childish exuberance.

149 leak

If you dream that your house leaks during a rainstorm, then questionable pleasure will come to a halt; an aberration will be uncovered.

150 snow

To see snow in a dream means that you are entering a period of inactivity; your attitude will determine whether the experience is restful or frustrating.

151 ice

Ice in a dream denotes that the passion in a relationship has begun to cool; if the ice is thawing then an issue that was keeping lovers apart will lose its significance.

152 hail

Hail suggests that someone who has wronged you feels regret and is seeking a way to make a reconciliation.

153 rain

If rain is accompanied by dark clouds, you feel apprehensive about a major commitment; however, a shower without clouds means that you feel invigorated by the challenges ahead.

154 volcano

A volcano relates to a fiery dispute within your household. If the volcano is smoking, the matter will remain unresolved; but if you see an eruption, a quarrel will clear the air.

155 earthquake

An earthquake is a message to take great care when completing a business deal or concluding a sale or purchase.

156 lightning

Lightning conveys an image of a sudden spark of creativity or insight that, if ignored, will be exploited by others whom you seek to emulate.

Thunder indicates feelings of doubt and fretfulness; it also relates to a figure of authority who wields excessive power.

158 landscape

A beautiful landscape or view is very positive unless it is viewed from inside, which indicates a strong feeling of detachment from the natural world.

159 vineyard

Dreaming of a vineyard indicates a balance between hard work and accepting the influence of forces beyond your control.

160 orchard

An orchard expresses life and new beginnings; to pick the fruit indicates eagerness to take your share of good fortune; if you are content to gather the windfalls you may be selling your talents too cheaply.

161 forest

A forest or wood is a powerful symbol of concealed fears and impulses; it may also relate to suppressed childhood ambitions.

162 spring

In a dream, spring represents youthful optimism and the birth of new ideas; it is also associated with cheerful companionship.

163 summer

Dreaming of summer foretells prosperity and fruitful relationships; summer also represents cosmic intelligence and justice.

164 winter

Dreaming of winter denotes material and spiritual gains after a period of rest and recuperation.

165 autumn

To dream of autumn denotes maturity verging on decline, a time of reckoning and change.

166 river

A dream involving a river is drawing attention to a need for renewal or a feeling of impermanence in your life.

167 canal

A canal is an ambiguous nature sign, because it is an artificial waterway that has the appearance of a river.

168 shells

To walk among or collect shells in your dream hints at extravagance and advancement at the expense of others. If the shells are broken, your folly will soon be stopped.

169 seaweed

When seaweed appears in your dream, it stands for a condition in which you are forced to improvise in order to rescue an unexpected and potentially embarrassing situation.

170 coral

Coral is a community of creatures that grows like a tree underwater; it is a complex symbol of family relationships and also has talismanic properties.

171 sea

Dreams of the sea reveal powerful unfulfilled needs; waves remind you that the momentum you need to realize your desires comes from trusting your own instincts.

172 tree

A tree is a symbol that links heaven and earth; it may express a need for spirituality or the serenity arising from putting someone else's needs before your own.

173 oak

An oak tree represents a powerful sense of being protected by those much older than you; it also encourages you to establish stability in your life.

174 acorns

Seeing acorns in your dream is a sign of enjoyment to come. If you collect them, you are storing up much happiness for the future; if you drop them, your plans will take a disappointing turn.

175 deciduous

A deciduous tree or shrub expresses a desire for renewal.

176 ash

An ash tree (or world tree) is a powerful symbol of resurrection associated with healing, strength, and justice; in a dream it is also connected to creativity and sensitivity.

177 alder

An alder tree (or tree of fire) can thrive in the wettest places; in a dream it signals the need for staying power and determination.

178 hawthorn

A hawthorn tree is associated with ancient spiritual energies and is a symbol of fertility; focus on your inner qualities and you will easily attract a partner.

179 hazel

A hazel tree represents distilled knowledge, truth, and honesty; in your dream it points to your powers of observation.

180 vine

A vine symbolizes joy and intoxication, but if you dream of one and are prone to changes of mood, you should seek mental stimulation and salubrious pleasures.

181 birch

A birch tree is synonymous with grace and beauty; it also refers to the cyclical nature of life's experiences.

182 elder

Elder represents the ability to see beyond the surface, and even the gift of prophecy; it highlights the need to remain receptive and eager to absorb information.

183 willow

To dream of a willow is to anticipate a sad journey during which you will enjoy the comfort and support of close friends.

184 maple

A maple tree represents the idea of sweetness being appreciated by one who has already tasted bitterness—joy discovered through adversity.

185 pine

The symbolic meaning of the pine tree is long life, celebration, and joy; it also encourages you to be mindful of your health and to maintain a positive outlook.

186 rowan

A rowan tree provides powerful protection against unwanted influences; you may be entering an uncertain period where you have to make up the rules as you go along.

The evergreen cypress tree is associated with the afterlife and paradise and is also a symbol of freedom; remain permanently attached to your vision of the future.

188 sycamore

The sycamore tree is related to the person that you wish to be. Who is standing under it?

189 tamarind

A tamarind tree denotes faithfulness and forbearance; good humor will become a strong business asset when you demonstrate restraint in the face of provocation.

Because chalk is chiefly composed of fossilized seashells, its presence in a dream represents the need to face unresolved sorrows; also acknowledging regrets through a steady transition.

Clay in a dream represents the expression of the imagination through action; begin a creative project immediately rather than waiting for inspiration.

Using a hoe suggests that your problems can be easily managed; if the weeds are out of control then you are attacking a problem from the wrong perspective.

193 rake

Using a rake indicates that your creativity will be allowed expression so long as you can convince others that your motives are in tune with theirs.

194 crops

A field of crops represents mental and physical growth; it also conveys a sense of completeness even if you have not yet finished what you set out to achieve.

195 smoke

To see smoke in a dream is an indication that someone is trying to warn you about possible danger ahead; proceed with caution and place greater importance on non-verbal cues.

196 meadow

Walking alone in a beautiful meadow represents your ability to depend upon yourself; it also suggests intellectual improvement through leisure.

197 mountain

To dream you are climbing a hill or mountain is good if you reach the summit, but if you fall or falter, you will be hindered by envy and lack of faith.

198 waterfall

A waterfall is a message that the objects of your wildest desires will be available; vitality and a feeling of renewal will help you view the world from a new perspective.

199 icicle

When a relationship ends, an icicle may appear in your dream as a symbol of dormant passion and cold beauty.

200 frost

Seeing frost in your dream indicates that you feel cold or indifferent to those around you; you feel constrained in your efforts to pursue an unbroken line of thought.

201 yucca

The pointed and rigid leaves of the yucca plant denote progress gained by thinking against the grain, as well as advancement through flexibility.

202 bark

Bark in your dream represents protection as well as irksome safeguards; beware of being too cautious when taking a risk.

203 roots

Roots in a dream represent waiting and patience; do not dig for treasure but wait for it to rise to the surface.

A thistle is for many a symbol of protection against invaders; in dream language it stands for persistent influence and the countering of strong criticism.

205 marigold

A marigold represents grief, despair, and melancholy; bright hopes will be dampened by news of a distracting nature.

206 magnolia

A magnolia is a symbol of perseverance; you may have to sacrifice your pleasure for the comfort of others.

207 bluebell

A bluebell represents constancy; your boldness will be rewarded with success if you stick to your original plans.

208 tulip

A yellow tulip represents hopeless love, but a tulip of any other color indicates fame and a declaration of devotion.

209 periwinkle

A blue periwinkle indicates early friendship, and a white periwinkle represents pleasant memories; you will enjoy the company of congenial friends.

210 geranium

A geranium denotes an expected meeting and an increase in prosperity; you may also enjoy unusual concessions in business.

211 garden

A dream about walking through a garden full of flowers and greenery is an expression of hopefulness and satisfaction; you feel empowered and fulfilled in your endeavors.

212 flowers

Fresh and beautiful flowers represent pleasure and profit; flowers that are withered and dying signify disappointment and grief.

213 grass

Grass is always a good sign; it signifies success in business, fame, and the possibility of romantic rapture.

214 bouquet

Getting flowers from someone is an indication
that your commitment to a project has not gone
unnoticed; you are appreciated even if recently
you have felt taken for granted.

215 poppies

Poppies suggest that you are
being distracted from your
goals by a temporary
indulgence; beware that instant
gratification does not make you
lose your focus.

216 jungle

Dreaming of a jungle indicates a state of
extreme anxiety or a hostile environment
that presents a variety of dangers.
You feel threatened on many fronts.

217 orchid

When an orchid makes an appearance
in your dream, it promises fertility and
creativity; it is also associated with purity
and its intense scent with ecstasy.

218 chrysanthemum

A chrysanthemum is a symbol
of harvest, rest, and ease; it also
represents hope and optimism.

219 peony

A peony is associated with secrecy;
its deep roots imply trust and reliability.
You will be expected to keep a promise
recently made, or a favor will be called in.

220 narcissus

To dream of narcissus is a warning that you may have been too inward-looking recently, and this may be frustrating your need to change.

221 sunflower

The sunflower represents loyalty, because its face always turns to follow the sun; it is also associated with longevity.

222 flowers

If flowers blossom in your dream, you can look forward to good times; if someone sends you flowers, you will have many admirers.

223 clover

To dream of clover is auspicious
and represents the fulfillment
of your desires and the arrival
of a period of prosperity.

224 daisy

A daisy is a flower of innocence
and childhood; it suggests that you
are searching for loyalty in love or
seeking solace in childish pursuits.

225 dahlia

A dahlia indicates that you will be
surrounded by people of elegance
and good taste; it also hints at
foreign travel.

226 heather

Heather or lavender expresses a need for solitude; if you feel fatigued, dreaming of these flowers invites you to devote more time to quiet pampering.

227 fern

A fern represents a secret bond of love; it is also linked to magic and suggests that your flamboyant side will make you sparkle if you trust your instincts.

228 hyacinth

A hyacinth represents prudence and forgiveness; it is up to you to make the first move to bring about a speedy reconciliation.

229 ivy

Ivy is a representation of a malign force in your life that is exploiting your good nature; it may also refer to your dogged persistence in the face of overwhelming opposition.

230 violet

A violet communicates modesty, faithfulness, and virtue; remaining true to your conscience will help you handle a difficult situation with calm diplomacy.

231 cactus

Dreaming of a cactus indicates your desire to repel unwanted attention; beware of closing yourself off to new experiences by appearing distant or aloof.

A red rose is a symbol of romantic passion and fulfillment; a rose with thorns denotes your hesitancy and ambiguous feelings in this area.

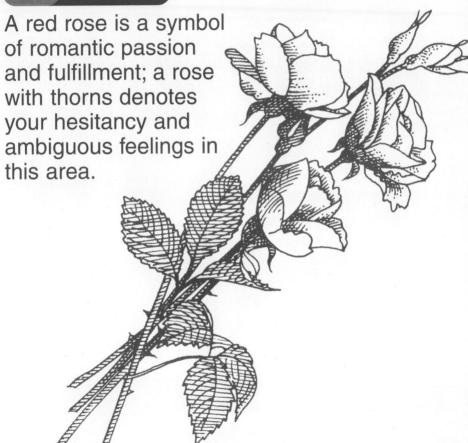

Peppermint is well known for its restorative properties; to dream of this herb implies that your good health and vitality will inspire the confidence of others.

234 snowdrop

A snowdrop is one of the first spring flowers and is a favorable dream image that suggests a new beginning after a period of inactivity.

235 daffodil

A daffodil is a symbol of hope and affection; it suggests that you will be surrounded with love in relation to a health issue.

236 honeysuckle

Honeysuckle is a symbol of lasting pleasure, permanence, and steadfastness; a sensuous encounter will bring good fortune in love.

237 shamrock

A shamrock is traditionally believed to provide protection against wild creatures such as snakes and scorpions, so if you see it in a dream, you may feel protected.

238 holly

Holly retains its berries during winter, and in a dream it indicates the power of patience, slow growth, and caution. Observe before attempting to change.

239 bamboo

Bamboo in a dream is a sign of growth and good luck, as well as spiritual development and knowledge through quiet reflection.

240 crocus

A crocus is a sign of protection against immoderate behavior; it is also associated with virtue and love. A substantial and lasting relationship may be threatened.

The nail-like leaves of the carnation
make it a powerful symbol of
spiritual passion in a dream;
it is also connected to betrothal
and fertility and may suggest
a romantic union.

242 dandelion

An ancient medicinal
plant, the dandelion is
closely connected to the
sun and healing through
the passage of time; let
go of negative feelings so
that painful memories
may gradually fade.

243 cedar

The natural strength and beauty of the cedar makes it an auspicious feature of a dream; its durability and longevity denote success and good health.

244 yew

Dreaming of a yew tree forewarns of illness and disappointment; if you are holding anger in your heart, you must let it go before it poisons your relationships.

245 nettles

If you walk through nettles without being stung, you will prosper; if you are stung you will feel unhappy about something that you have failed to achieve, which is causing you much regret.

246 bay leaves

Bay leaves in a dream represent consistency; a bay tree is a symbol of glory, and a bay wreath indicates that your excellence will soon be rewarded.

247 palm

Palm trees in your dream promise exotic experiences and are an emblem of victory, success, and joy; expect happiness in abundance.

248 mistletoe

Mistletoe represents powers of healing and foretells celebrations; to dream of mistletoe—which is associated with immortality—is a sign of great insight.

Dreaming of lilies
indicates much sadness
and physical suffering.

The Animal Kingdom

To hear a cock crowing in the morning is a positive sign of youthful energy; at nighttime it's a sign that you're harboring regrets. Fighting indicates family tensions.

Hens or chickens indicate that you may be motivated by petty desires that threaten your dignity and inner balance; resolve to approach your dealings with simplicity and sincerity.

252   rooster

A rooster is a proud bird that warns against ignoring the part that luck may have played in your successes; approach others with humility when offering advice and accept their counsel with good grace.

253   nightingale

If a nightingale sings in your dreams, you can look forward to some happy news, especially in your love life or family relationships.

254 magpie

A magpie denotes dissatisfaction, disputes, and domestic unhappiness; several magpies mean that your hurts will be multiplied if you continue to favor people within your own circle.

255 birds flying

Birds flying overhead suggest that prosperity awaits you if you progress calmly with a continuous movement; birdsong corresponds to mental clarity and quickness of perception.

256 buzzard

If you dream of a buzzard feeding off old bones you may have skeletons in your closet; if the bird flies away, you still have time to make amends.

257   eagle

An eagle is a sign that good fortune and prosperity will result from clear and decisive action, but first you must accept counsel from experienced advisers.

258   parrot

A parrot represents idle chatter and gossip; if someone passes your ideas off as her own, you must take action to make certain that your contribution is acknowledged.

259   cuckoo

Seeing a cuckoo indicates feelings of displacement or alienation; if you cultivate gainful relationships, you will overcome any feelings of disaffection.

260 swans

White swans floating upon calm water foretell prosperous outlooks and fruitful experiences; they also symbolize the blindness of love.

261 dove

A dove is a well-known symbol of peace and also denotes home building and a favorable domestic situation characterized by gentleness and conciliation.

262 pigeon

Dreaming about a pigeon is a sign that you are being held responsible for the actions of others.

263 blackbird

A blackbird means temptation and seduction; if the bird is singing, you will face a situation where your values may be compromised.

264 peacock

A peacock uses its impressive tail feathers to attract a mate; if you dream of this bird, you risk wasting energy through flamboyant displays and proud behavior.

265 pelican

A pelican represents parental devotion; you will advance your own cause by helping those around you fulfill their immediate needs.

266 penguin

A flightless penguin may be a sign that you are arrogantly trying to fly beyond your power; do not boast of your accomplishments.

267 crow

A crow is a symbol of monogamy and is also linked to battles in Celtic myth; if you dream of one, you should put aside a superficial union to seek worthwhile company.

268 albatross

When an albatross appears in your dream, stormy weather will approach.

269 ostrich

An ostrich represents justice and truth and is also a symbol of meditation; if you respect natural laws, others will spontaneously be drawn to your cause.

The cliff-nesting seagull appears in your dream as a symbol of the conflict between self-preservation and exploration; think multidimensionally rather than settling for easy answers and formulas.

The iridescent humming bird darts around in your dream to represent ideas made brilliant by rapid action; beware of beating your wings so fast that you fail to move forward.

A flamingo stands for gregarious enjoyment of new experiences; do not be afraid of trying something new.

An owl represents inner knowledge and silent wisdom; it often makes an appearance in a dream to highlight the good fortune that results from patient anticipation.

274 raven

A croaking raven is a symbol of pillaging and greedy consumption; selfishness may be lowering your dignity and making you behave in a self-indulgent way.

275 skylark

Noted for its singing while in flight, the skylark encourages you to be fired up with an enthusiastic idea and to pursue freedom with reckless abandon.

276 sparrow

A sparrow denotes offerings made by the very poor and highlights the need to exploit even a meager talent with generosity of spirit.

277 swallow

A graceful swallow represents the delaying of gratification; it also corresponds to the spring and a journey of spiritual growth.

278 crane

The crane is associated with long life and purity; if you dream of a crane, be realistic and maintain your poise and modesty in order to pursue a long-term goal.

279 thrush

The thrush, with its spotted breast and melodious song, may appear in your dream to highlight the idea of using senses that have been neglected or underestimated.

280 robin

A robin is a symbol of courage and natural innocence; its appearance in your dream suggests a need to act without contrivance or self-interest.

When a duck makes an appearance in your dream, it suggests a fortunate journey that may involve traveling across water; expect to ascend to a new level of influence.

282 butterflies

A dream involving
butterflies signifies
creativity and romance;
it indicates that by
looking after your
inner self you
will accomplish
a significant
transformation.

283 moth

Dreaming of a moth highlights the
need to compensate for a personal
shortcoming by moderating your
approach to a hastily conceived
plan or business contract.

Mosquitoes indicate that somebody has been monopolizing much of your time and resources by his or her refusal to face facts that are obvious to everyone else.

285 caterpillar

Dreaming of a caterpillar means that you will find yourself in an embarrassing situation in which assertive action will be futile.

286 ants

Ants represent preoccupation with trifling worries; they also represent diligence and forging practical alliances to achieve an ambitious undertaking.

287 cocoon

To see a cocoon in your dream is an auspicious reminder of the feelings of fragility and vulnerability that you will inevitably experience during a period of transformation or maturity.

288 cricket

A cricket lays its eggs in the ground and reaches the surface a mature insect; therefore it appears in your dream as a symbol of death and resurrection.

To dream of a snail expresses your need to retreat to safety in order to rediscover your inner light; it also denotes slow but steady progress toward your goals.

290 locust

If the voracious and destructive locust appears in your dream, it signifies a disruption in your prosperity that is linked to migration or travel.

291 worm

A worm is a symbol of the acceptance of imperfections; it encourages you to treat all aspects of your life as integral parts of your development.

292 flies

Seeing flies in your dream indicates feelings of remorse or the abrupt failure of a scheme. If you trap a fly, you will regain lost affections. Flies also correspond to sickness.

A hovering dragonfly indicates that you are close to realizing great fortune as long as you are not daunted by the effort required to ensure success.

If you see fish swimming in clear waters, you will be favored by those in positions of power. If you catch fish, you will acquire wealth through your own ingenuity.

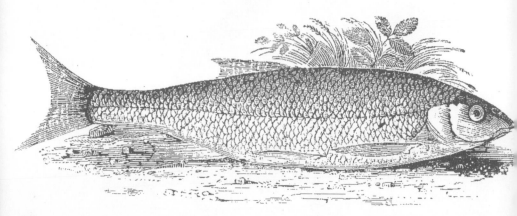

295 trout

A trout is a sign of abundant fortune;
to dream of catching one indicates great
competence and skill in physical pursuits.

296 crab

A crab in your dream implies that you
may be seeking protection by
withdrawing into your shell or by
sidestepping important issues.

297 octopus

If you are struggling with several
priorities, the many-legged octopus may
appear in your dream to suggest that
you should simplify and practice
moderation as a matter of principle.

298 barnacles

Barnacles indicate that hesitation will lead to the accumulation of debt or obstacles; address an important issue before it becomes a burden.

299 salmon

The salmon is a symbol of security and permanence; seeing one in a dream indicates that you are dependable and constant during a time of upheaval.

300 catfish

A catfish, with its barbels or "whiskers," is something of an oddity; in your dream it signifies the arrival of a mysterious stranger whose true nature will not be immediately apparent.

The slippery eel appears in your dream to signal evasive action; you may dissolve a bond or distance yourself from a group.

302 goldfish

A goldfish is a symbol of good fortune, prosperity, and beauty; to see one in your dream suggests that completing something will bring you natural harmony.

303 tuna

A tuna represents extreme agility, stamina, and a long journey; if one features in your dream, it shows that you will become more accomplished as you transform experience into character.

304 seal

To see a seal in your dream may be a sign that you are blaming yourself for failing to reach an impossible goal.

305 school of fish

A school of fish indicates that you are becoming involved with too many people and projects that are draining your resources; seek the company of compatible people.

306 dolphin

The intelligent and agile dolphin appears as a healer and guide in your dream; to ride a dolphin signifies harmony and innocent intentions.

307 shark

A shark signifies thriving without continuous motion; if you have been feeling restless, remember that there is more to life than increasing its speed.

308 crocodile

A crocodile lives on both land and water and in some cultures is associated with carrying the whole world on its back; accepting too many responsibilities will make you a servant to many instead of a master.

309 caribou

The migrating caribou is almost constantly on the move; when it features in your dream it highlights a challenge regarding the managing of change.

310 chameleon

If a chameleon appears in your dream, it suggests that you are undergoing a period of instability; temporary uncertainty is not failure if the final goal is kept in mind.

Because of the lizard's attraction to the sun, dreaming of this creature indicates that you will enjoy constant renewal and bask in the warmth of true friendship.

A tortoise indicates being drawn back to where you belong, and resting between moments of struggle.

The hippopotamus is a sign of a voracious appetite and the application of unreasonable force; gather friends with genuine enthusiasm rather than shows of conspicuous consumption.

314 toad

A toad or frog indicates that peace runs the risk of turning into stagnation; beware of resting when you should be taking action.

315 lemmings

Dreaming of lemmings denotes a dangerous situation; if they appear in your dream, they may be warning you against taking risks.

316 otter

An otter is a symbol of the wily hunter that strikes without warning; look out for unforeseen changes.

317 snake

A snake coils in repose or arches before it attacks, so when it appears in a dream, it is a symbol of untapped creative or amorous energy.

318 polar bear

A polar bear is often a good omen, but it may also be a warning that false friends are holding you back or threatening your peace of mind.

319 gazelle

A gazelle denotes beauty, grace, and gentleness; you will enjoy an enchanting amorous encounter.

320 stampede

If you witness a stampede of animals in your dream, it suggests that your ability to hold your ground in the face of public opinion will soon be tested.

To see a stag in your dream indicates that you are surrounded by honest and supportive friends and that your social life is enjoyable.

322 leopard

When a leopard appears in your dream, it expresses aggression and pride; a wild leap may give you swift advancement, which you must accept with humility.

323 lion

Subduing a lion shows that you are determined to overcome obstacles in your life; if it overpowers or bites you, then you are struggling with your challenges.

324 zebra

The appearance of a zebra in your dream suggests that you need to focus your energy in one direction.

325 tiger

A tiger is a fearsome predator that sneaks up on you unawares; it expresses your anxiety about unforeseen or imagined obstacles.

elephant

When an elephant features in your dream, it indicates you are laying a firm foundation for achieving wealth or great honors.

A coyote is a pragmatist; take time to address issues in a practical manner. If this animal appears in your dream, your mind may be telling you to apply yourself patiently to the solving of a problem.

328 monkeys

Dreaming of monkeys represents the impish side of your personality, but it may also be a message that some people wish to trick you with flattery.

329 meerkat

A meerkat can eat a scorpion without getting poisoned, which makes it a potent dream image of protection against malign forces and corruption.

330 mongoose

A mongoose is a symbol of wealth, luck, and prosperity; it is also a reminder that wealth brings responsibilities.

331 anteater

An anteater may be a warning against causing unnecessary damage to get what you want; subtlety will bring greater rewards.

A moose often kicks forward with its front hooves when it attacks; in a dream it represents the need to face a problem head on or make a tough choice with directness.

333 rhinoceros

A rhinoceros indicates the single-mindedness that you must possess to reach your destination.

Buffaloes signify powerful adversaries; you must use diplomacy and wit to bend them to your will, instead of trying to match their physical strength.

335 camel

A camel is a beast of burden that has great patience and determination. It encourages you to draw on your inner resources to deal with an impending crisis or disappointment.

336 bear

Being chased or attacked by a bear in a dream symbolizes aggression, and fierce competition in all areas of activity.

337 bobcat

The bobcat is a small animal with a fearsome growl; it appears in your dream to denote your desire to raise your status or persuade others of your importance.

A kangaroo attacking you in your dream means that your reputation is being threatened; if it is friendly then the nurturing aspect of your personality is being underused.

339 **deer**

When the fragile and beautiful deer enters your dream, you will enjoy pure and profound friendships; hunting the deer indicates that you feel unworthy of another's affections.

340 **panda**

A panda is a solitary and fastidious animal; dreaming of one represents your need for privacy or confidentiality in a family situation.

341 **fox**

A fox prowling about in your dream represents quickness of thought. You must use your intuition and intellect to resolve an issue; remain watchful and bide your time.

342   wolf

A wolf in your dream represents fierce
independence and a predatory search
for self-fulfillment; you may also
experience a misunderstanding through
your desire for solitude.

343   mole

If a mole appears in your dream, it
indicates secret adversaries—all the
more reason for you to cultivate your
inner qualities and allow them to
influence everything you do.

344 boar

A boar signifies fearlessness in battle;
you may be involved in a dispute or
standoff in which your bluff is called.

345 hyena

The scavenging hyena is the epitome of cowardly
behavior; you cannot expect to coast much
longer if you have
left others to
do all the
hard work.

squirrel

Squirrels signify the need to let
go of something that is becoming
a burden; they also represent
the need to move cautiously in
preparation for hard times ahead.

347 rabbit

A rabbit represents good luck; a white
rabbit means you are right to trust the
faithfulness of a loved one.

If a rabbit runs away or escapes from you, you will lose something of value in unusual circumstances; if you capture a hare, you will win a contest or find something you thought was lost.

A horse indicates that things will take shape on their own accord; beware of monopolizing your power and continue to work constructively with others.

350 pony

A pony signifies that you should seek the support of a strong and reliable helper; do not attempt great changes at this time.

351 lambs

Lambs denote meekness, tolerance, and self-sacrifice. By working silently and unobtrusively for a noble cause, you will avoid confusion and conflict.

352 sheep

Dreaming of sheep indicates that everyone has a function and contributes to the whole; share your insights with those who are ready to listen.

When a bull appears in your dream, your passions may be out of control; if you rise above a stressful situation and remain emotionally detached, others will follow your example.

goats

Dreaming of goats means that you
may have to use considerable force
to remove an obstacle in
your way; remain flexible
and resist the
temptation to settle
for a clumsy
temporary solution.

355 porcupine

A porcupine is a symbol of the warrior in repose;
if you are in a position of power, look at your
abilities and consider whether what you intend to
do is right and whether it may be too early to act.

356 groundhog

A groundhog is the symbol of winter's midpoint, and its appearance in your dream may correspond with an important decision regarding the beginning of a new cycle of growth.

357 pig

A pig is a warning that if you move clumsily and impulsively, you will exhaust your energies and risk jeopardizing a carefully thought-out strategy.

A donkey represents stubborn determination. However, if your steadfastness is being misinterpreted as martyrdom, consider whether your inflexibility is alienating possible allies.

A cat denotes unhappiness and bad luck; your self-reliance may blind you to your weak areas unless you correct your own faults instead of pointing them out in others.

Rats signify feelings of guilt or envy.
They may also represent deceit and
secrecy. If they run away, you will be
able to outwit your opponents with
advance warning or treachery.

A dream of mice highlights
domestic troubles or trouble in
business. If you see a mouse
wearing clothes, you may
be heading for a
scandalous revelation.

If a dog features in your dream, you will enjoy loyalty and generosity from your friends; a barking dog heralds unexpected news, and a growling dog means you may be punishing others for your own mistakes.

363 puppy

A puppy represents playfulness and blithe friendships; it also indicates the deepening of friendship through the sharing of lighthearted pursuits.

364 ferret

The ferret is a predator of snakes and rodents; when one appears in your dream it represents protection against betrayal or an untimely romantic liaison.

365 bat

A bat is a symbol of immortality and intelligence but also of the inversion of the natural order and of melancholy influences; it is often associated with envy and the keeping of secrets.

366 COWS

A herd of cows with full udders indicates prosperity and fulfillment of wishes and desires.

367 calf

A calf denotes sacrifice and trust; your sincerity may be called into question, or a union based on ulterior motives will be dissolved.

368 beaver

A dream involving a beaver indicates self-criticism and even self-sabotage; consider whether you are undermining your own efforts and inviting failure.

369 shrew

Seeing a shrew represents working
constructively with others in an informal
context and without deep commitment.

370 badger

To dream of a badger denotes success after
a long period of stalemate or hardship.

The odorous defense employed by the skunk makes its appearance in your dream a cause for concern; beware of imposing your tastes on an unwilling stranger.

372 sloth

A sloth is a symbol of the value of life lived at a slower pace; if it appears in your dream, it may be a call to reduce your needs rather than increase your acquisition.

373 opossum

An opossum's ability to fend off attackers by pretending to be dead makes it an interesting dream symbol; it suggests that you may have to resort to unconventional tactics when concluding a business deal.

374 koala

Thriving on eucalyptus leaves, the koala signifies self-sufficiency and meticulous attention to detail.

375 raccoon

Noted for its humanlike paws, the raccoon appears in your dream to highlight your need to see others as equals rather than as sounding boards.

Food and Drink

376 social eating

Because eating is such a social activity, dreaming of eating alone indicates feelings of loneliness; eating with others denotes the support of reliable friends.

377 overeating

Overeating is inauspicious if accompanied by feelings of guilt; take care that you are not acting outside your legitimate sphere of influence or power.

378 interrupted eating

If you dream of being interrupted during eating, or of feeling unsatisfied and hungry, your resources may be stretched beyond their limits.

379 breakfast

Breakfast is indicative of new beginnings;
conversely, it may be a sign that an old
project is demanding more of your attention
than you had anticipated initially.

380 picnic

Dreaming of a picnic might correspond to your
wish that some part of your life be more relaxed
and informal than convention has allowed; it may
also indicate that simplicity can improve your
friendship prospects.

381 vitamins

If vitamins feature in your dream, they
represent the unlearning of negative
patterns; you may need to start putting
your health before worldly concerns.

Consuming soup illustrates the dreamer's attraction to spontaneity; it may also reveal that a more cautious approach will lead to better results than an impulsive desire for instant results.

383 salad

To dream of eating salad suggests that you may be approaching something that is causing you anxiety by playing it safe; it expresses extreme caution and a fear of betrayal.

384 canned food

Dreaming of canned food is a sign that you are reaching your limits; you may have grown beyond the need for guidance from a trusted adviser.

385 pie

If you eat a pie in your dream, you require more clarity of thought in order to disentangle yourself from an unsettling and inauspicious union.

386 oysters

Eating oysters in your dream expresses the urgent need for equanimity in relation to a matter of a delicate nature; it may also suggest an invasion of your privacy.

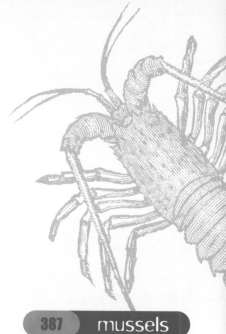

387 mussels

Dreaming of mussels refers to gathering together for mutual prosperity; every thought and word will influence your well-being in a social context.

Eating lobsters expresses the dreamer's ambivalence concerning a conflict that demands decisive action or extreme measures to prevent it from spiraling out of control.

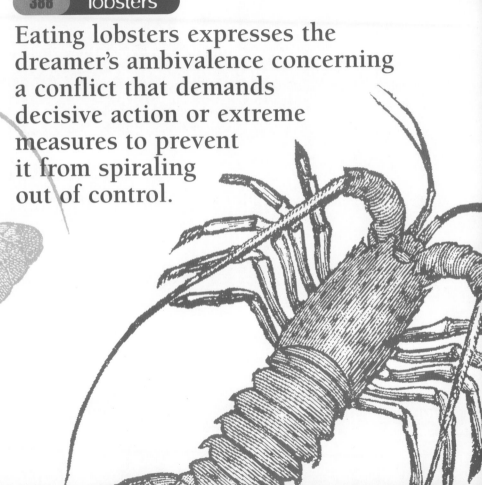

389 raw meat

Dreaming of raw meat indicates that something emotionally sensitive in your life has recently been exposed in the public domain; it also represents inexperience and immaturity.

390 sausages

Sausages denote tedious routine and the need for greater challenges and variety in your social or business affairs.

391 organ meats

To see or eat organ meats or leftovers in a dream indicates that you may be thinking about a choice previously made; you may be regretting a decision or wishing to revisit an unresolved issue.

When gravy features in your dream, it indicates that hospitality can become an irksome burden; a family member may thwart an established ritual.

393   hot dog

Eating a hot dog or burger is a sign of beguiling activities, uncontrolled indulgence, and the gratification of overwhelming desires.

394   onions

A dream involving onions corresponds to feelings of envy or ill will that come your way as a consequence of your achievements; it may also be a call for greater sensitivity and humility.

395   carrots

Dreaming of carrots portends financial dividends resulting from a solid investment; you will receive the promise of a tempting reward.

396   parsnip

A parsnip makes an appearance in your dream to warn against setting down roots without first being sure of your surroundings.

397   turnip

A turnip is redolent of wholesome fulfillment and the sharing of material comforts; the dreamer may soon enjoy renewed effort after a temporary setback.

To dream of chives means that you will interact easily and positively with others; your personality will radiate a subtle inner harmony.

399 olives

Olives indicate friendly companionship and a return to mellow equilibrium; it is also symbolic of peace and healing.

400 cabbages

When cabbages appear in a dream, it forewarns of unfaithfulness in love and general disorder; also the dreamer may be troubled by unexpected bills.

okra

Okra suggests enchanting warmth and enlightenment; fried okra corresponds to a family gathering or celebration.

spinach

Eating spinach is a sign of a healthy and untroubled life; a child will bring laughter and great strength.

potatoes

Potatoes indicate reliability and convention and an acceptance of one's limitations; they may also represent indolence and complacency influencing an ardent emotional attachment.

404 leeks

To dream of leeks refers to the gradual stripping away of power or influence; you may be required to prove your competence or restate your position.

405 yam

The yam is a life-sustaining symbol of kinship and commonality; within the family it expresses a need to foster a sense of responsibility for each other's welfare.

406 garlic

Eating garlic in a dream symbolizes vitality and gregarious enjoyment; it also evokes a desire for protection and may warn against placing too much emphasis on superstitious preoccupations.

407 mushrooms

Mushrooms denote the accumulation of wealth through speculative enterprises; you may be required to circumvent conventional paths in order to prosper.

408 cauliflower

When a cauliflower features in a dream, it signifies that the dreamer's active participation in events or activities will be sought from all sides; acceptance will bring pleasing benefits.

409 peppers

Dreaming of peppers, you should be wary of danger; you may have to change your plans because of the anger and resistance of others.

If you eat mustard in your dream, you will be chastised or corrected; if you feel guilty about your actions, forgive yourself and move on.

Cinnamon stands for tokens of friendship between lovers or friends; you will receive a gift from a loved one.

A dream involving nutmeg relates to a warm home and the display of wealth; if you are planning an important social gathering, aim for comfort rather than ostentation.

413 fennel

Fennel is a symbol of victory and appears in your dream to represent success; you will reach your goal after many attempts.

414 parsley

Parsley represents moderation during a celebration; if you attend a party you will maintain your dignity despite raucous festivity.

415 tarragon

If tarragon appears in your dream, it will protect you against a person who seems to offer only persistent criticism.

Basil, the king of plants, features in your dream to signal that royalty will exert an influence over you in the near future.

417 coriander

Coriander is a symbol of spiritual awareness and protection; a family member will spread happiness and encouragement.

418 cumin

Cumin is a symbol of greed and meanness; if you dream of this spice, you should examine your motives and reconsider an answer given in haste.

419 beets

Eating beets symbolizes cheerful optimism in the face of hardship; if the dreamer is sanguine at all times, he or she will rise to prominence during a crisis.

420 celery

Dreaming of celery signifies that you feel that recent results do not justify the effort you have expended; you may receive an unsatisfactory return on an investment.

421 gourd

To dream of the quick-growing gourd represents fertility but also warns against wasting resources to achieve fast results; allow the right associations to form naturally and spontaneously.

422 vinegar

Vinegar signifies a contract or agreement entered into unwillingly; however, disruptive elements will soon dissipate and order will be restored.

423 avocado

The avocado has a stone at the center of its delicate flesh and symbolizes gentle persuasion with a solid conviction of purpose.

424 artichoke

An artichoke resembles a burning torch and appears in your dream to signify your desire to accept a challenge.

To dream of cloves represents increased involvement in an enterprise; your ideas will be fruitless if they are not put into immediate action.

426   radishes

Eating radishes in a dream denotes stimulating intellectual pursuits and sharp wit; you may encounter a person of unusual grace or erudition.

427   ginger

If you consume ginger in your dream you are rejecting unkind criticism; listen only to those who advise you out of love and respect.

198

428 asparagus

Dreaming of asparagus indicates aspirations to power and wealth; it also expresses the dreamer's desire for an enigmatic reputation and the company of exclusive associates.

429 cucumber

To dream of a cucumber denotes health and well-being; it also indicates success resulting from sticking to one's principles.

430 kohlrabi

To eat kohlrabi in a dream refers to maturity achieved through acceptance of life's difficulties; resist a desire to burden others with your grievances.

431 salt

To dream of salt suggests that you will be introduced to someone with a sharp and lively wit who will add zest to your social dealings.

432 pepper

Dreaming of pepper indicates that a domestic conflict will clear the air and lead to greater understanding.

433 sugar

A dream in which sugar is featured speaks about fellowship and the sharing of common interests in an informal context.

In a dream hummus may represent a family gathering in which your hospitality and generosity will be under close scrutiny.

435 honey

Honey brings good luck and the opportunity to acquire considerable wealth and love without one overshadowing the other.

436 lentils

Lentils represent the need to draw upon inner reserves during a time of hardship; sincerity will save you from making careless mistakes.

To dream of beans signifies the disclosing of a secret or misdirected activity yielding disappointing results; dried beans mean dissatisfaction with secular matters.

438　peas

Dreaming of eating peas represents attainment of wealth; it is also a reminder that when several people are motivated by a common goal, they can achieve prosperity together.

439   rice

Rice is a sign of success and friendship, especially domestic bliss; rice that has fallen on the floor or become dirty hints at separation or sacrifice.

440   couscous

Seeing couscous in your dream denotes that when your adversaries stand together, you must confront them one by one to make them yield to your will.

441   spaghetti

Dreaming of spaghetti or noodles indicates a desire to disentangle yourself from an intricate situation.

442 doughnuts

Doughnuts suggest a welcome break from routine, but be on your guard for those who seek to entice you with trivial promises.

443 tomatoes

If you eat tomatoes in your dream, you may be neglecting to right an injustice or you may unwittingly be contributing to an undesirable status quo; throwing tomatoes expresses resistance and direct action.

444 oats

Dreaming of oats suggests a need to placate someone to smooth over an unsettling problem; now is not the time to make waves.

Dreaming of hops refers to failure
through laziness; if you redouble
your efforts, you will soon rise
above adversity.

446 cereal

A dream of cereal or grain
represents life-sustaining
nourishment by following
in the steps of one's
ancestors; tradition is
currently a dominant
influence in your waking life.

447 raisins

Because raisins are dried grapes, their appearance in a dream signifies the frustration of hopes or a feeling of regret after a period of nearsighted indulgence.

448 grapes

Dreaming of grapes may be related to passionate, short-lived relationships; it may also be an invitation to seize the pleasures of the moment.

449 chestnuts

Eating chestnuts means you may be remembering a loss; it also signifies that if your outlook is narrow, you will misread important signals and miss a much-anticipated opportunity.

450 coconut

Eating a coconut in a dream suggests that exotic pleasures will reward your resourcefulness and tenacity; you may embark on a venture that calls for versatility or learning new skills.

451 almonds

Almonds imply wealth in store even if this good fortune is accompanied by moments of sadness.

452 walnuts

A dream involving walnuts corresponds to your need for protection through a period of transition; it can also express inner decisiveness and the courage to let go of outmoded aspects.

453 cherries

To dream of cherries indicates a desire to indulge your whims and caprices and ignore the consequences.

454 banana

A banana tree has wind-torn leaves, so if you see a banana in your dream, it is a symbol of the impermanence of all things, and of wise contemplation.

455 pomegranate

Consuming a pomegranate in your dream means that an embellished account or explanation with a mysterious or fascinating quality will distract you or hinder your progress.

The slow-growing and long-lived blueberry denotes accomplishment through persistence and constancy of purpose; it also represents versatility and a healthy outlook.

457   apples

A dream involving apples brings good luck and the acquiring of knowledge; you are valued by those around you and can expect wise counsel.

458   figs

Figs are augurs of fertility and abundance, but they may also warn against accepting the triviality and platitudes of others.

459 pear

Spherical at its base but tapering toward the stem, a pear denotes fluctuating fortune; you may need to employ other talents to compensate for weakness in one area.

460 gooseberries

Dreaming of gooseberries indicates anticipation or even intuition; it also warns against taking a result for granted.

461 papaya

When struck, the papaya makes a characteristic hollow sound; if it appears in your dream it represents speaking without knowledge or experience.

462 fruit salad

Dreaming of fruit salad indicates a healthy balance of intelligence and insight; a fresh approach will help you solve a disagreement.

463 nectarine

A nectarine in a dream is a symbol of long life and immortality; it is also a sign that your self-esteem does not rely on outward appearances, but on appropriate thoughts and actions.

464 orange

An orange appearing in a dream is a potent symbol of female leadership; it also evokes the sunrise or sunset and the arrival of significant change.

465 apricot

Eating an apricot denotes practicality and creativity; it may also indicate lack of self-worth and a need for popularity. Guard against flitting from person to person and invest in making strong connections.

466 peach

A peach represents fertility and is also a symbol of purity and even immortality; to eat this fruit in a dream indicates the need for productivity and transparency in all your dealings.

467 mango

A mango is a powerful symbol of creation, new life, and refreshing change after a period of drought; it may also denote a blessing in disguise.

468 passion fruit

Eating passion fruit in a dream is connected to forgiveness and mastery of your emotions; recognize that those around you are motivated by the same human desires as yourself.

469 melons

Melons symbolize hope and throwing off unnecessary commitments; expect an unusual resolution to an irksome problem.

470 strawberry

With its graceful form and pure color, a strawberry is a symbol of perfect righteousness and continuous life; a sacrifice on your part will bring immense pleasure that will touch countless others.

213

471 star fruit

If you dream of the golden-ribbed star fruit or carambola, you will be surrounded by wealthy strangers who will bring you good fortune.

472 raspberries

If you dream of raspberries, you may be harboring remorse; if you eat them in your dream, you are being encouraged to offer submissive respect or make a humble apology.

473 grapefruit

The eating of grapefruit in your dream signifies that a misunderstanding will arise between business and family commitments, and indicates the need for greater communication.

474 plum

A plum is a symbol of mutual consent; you must gain the trust of everybody in the group if you expect to lead them.

475 eating plums

Eating plums indicates flirtatious behavior and a desire to attract attention.

476 pizza

A dream involving pizza is an expression of welcome and warmth; allow your youthful exuberance to guide your actions.

477 eggs

Eggs have always represented new beginnings and the spark of creation. To break eggs hints at an unavoidable sacrifice.

478 cheese

Eating cheese denotes much sorrow and unhappiness; if you slice the cheese, you risk alienating others with your insensitivity.

479 chocolate

Whenever chocolate appears in your dream, you can be sure that you are a good provider for those who depend on you; if it is bitter, you may be heading for disappointment.

480   bread

Eating bread is a powerful symbol of life; stale or moldy bread signifies a need to be mindful of your core values.

481   pancakes

Making or eating pancakes suggests that times ahead will require thriftiness and resourcefulness; tossing pancakes indicates courageous acceptance of a challenge.

482   lard

Dreaming of lard or butter signifies that you should remain vigilant and objective during a meeting with those in a position of power or of great wealth.

483 flour

Dreaming of flour draws attention to
your creativity and innate potential,
because flour is an essential ingredient
in making many other delicious foods.

484 ice cream

When ice cream appears in your dream it
represents your desire to feel pampered;
it may also indicate feelings of guilt about
overindulgence or excessive fastidiousness.

485 biscuits

**Biscuits forewarn of the disintegration of
a close relationship; baking biscuits
indicates your desire to heal a rift.**

486 coffee

To dream of coffee indicates that you may have been led astray by an adversary who seeks to undermine your peace of mind; if you grind coffee you are harboring a grudge.

487 irish coffee

To dream that you are making Irish coffee means that a colleague may pull strings for your advancement; to drink it indicates success in business and matters requiring diplomacy.

488 tea

When you brew tea in a dream, future indiscretions will make you sorry; to spill tea is a sign of domestic uncertainty and tension.

489 champagne

To drink champagne in your dream is a warning to rein in your expenses; if it spills, your finances are already in disarray.

490 wine

Wine represents esoteric knowledge and joyful abundance; drinking wine from the bottle represents reckless behavior or a secret love.

491 alcohol

Dreaming of alcohol represents the attraction of opposites; a surprise encounter will lead to an unusual romantic liaison.

A cup is a symbol of maternal nourishment and salvation; if you share a cup in your dream, it expresses your solidarity and fidelity, or acceptance of a universal idea.

Cutlery is a symbol of the triumph of the social contract over baser instincts; it appears in your dream to warn against immoderate or antisocial behavior.

A ladle appearing in your dream indicates family solidarity during hardship; it also signifies the strong sticking up for the weaker members of a group.

A saucepan is a symbol of a well-run household; if you dream of a saucepan when you are away from home, it means you should enjoy the little things that make you happy.

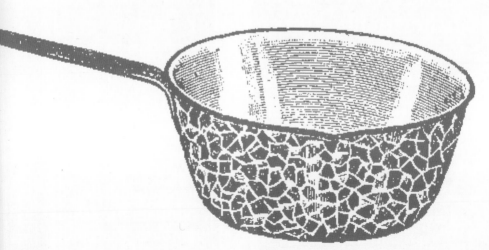

496 rolling pin

A rolling pin represents accomplishment within the household; if it is covered in flour, you will be surrounded by young children.

497 kettle

A kettle appears in a dream to suggest that you are withholding your true feelings out of a sense of obligation to a group or adherence to a cause.

498 thermos

A thermos corresponds to the bearing of a grudge; you may be required to take a short journey to repair a relationship.

A well-stocked refrigerator alludes to feelings of hospitality toward a visitor; if it is empty, a relative will overstay his or her welcome.

500 oven

An oven appears in your dream during a time of difficult change; just as clay must be fired to become hard, a difficult experience will fire your beliefs and make them more durable.

Universal
Symbols

501   **1**

The number one corresponds to individuality and creativity; it may also hint that the dreamer is being selfish in relation to the subject matter of the dream.

502   **2**

The number two denotes balance, sharing, and communication; it invites you to examine these themes in relation to the subject matter of the dream.

503   **3**

The number three corresponds to mind, body, and spirit, and suggests a sense of completeness; it is strongly related to commitment and the heart.

The number four, like a square or box, stands for containment or restriction.

The number five represents sensuality and your five senses; it also relates to your destiny and to change.

The number six represents compassion and the power to go beyond the five senses; it is also associated with conflict.

507 7

The number seven corresponds to your spiritual development; like the number three it symbolizes completeness.

508 8

The number eight indicates expansion through balance, as well as infinity or eternity; like the number four it expresses wholeness of being.

509 9

The number nine is another symbol of completeness, like the numbers three and seven, but it pertains to your life purpose and your long-term objectives.

510 "zero"

Zero is the perfect symbol with no beginning or end; it represents God and your ideals.

511 large numbers

Large numbers appearing in your dream are often indicative of a restless mind and anxious thoughts concerning finance. It may be time for a well-earned break.

512 color

Color is there to heal you and to guide you; it is an expression of your reaction to what you encounter in your dreams.

513 red

Red expresses fun and sexuality on the one hand, aggression on the other. It encourages you to seek fulfillment.

514 green

Green expresses a need for reconciliation, for healing and harmony. It invites you to examine areas of your life that are out of balance.

Pink is associated with a need for unconditional love, usually from a parental figure. It draws you back to the nurturing protection of your family.

Yellow personifies the intellect and mental activity.

Orange represents energy and vitality and often relates to your career, creativity, healing, and the release of mental and emotional blocks.

518   blue

Blue relates to the spiritual and
philosophical aspects of your life;
dark blue is associated with superstition,
and light blue with hope and faith.

519   purple

**Purple is a symbol of authority and leadership;
if this color appears in your dream, it may
mean that you should examine the power
structures that influence your waking life.**

520   gray

Gray is a color that expresses
uncertainty, clouded judgment, and
disquiet; it can also correspond to an
area of emotional denial or equivocation.

521   brown

Brown bespeaks practicality and a sense of being grounded, as well as self-discipline and the potential for growth.

522   turquoise

Embodying the spirits of the sea and the sky, turquoise is an important color that symbolizes your individuality and your humor.

523   silver

When silver features in your dreams, you are being asked to examine the extent to which your intuitive powers are being used or neglected.

524   gold

Gold in dreams corresponds to your ability to heal yourself or others through spiritual tolerance and understanding.

525   sun

Dreaming of the sun reflects your aspirations and position in society; you will prosper in business and gain much needed insight.

526   sunrise

Dreaming of a sunrise corresponds to nurturing power and the illumination of your goals.

527   sunset

To see the sunset points to the end of a period of well-being and security. It warns you to approach the future with confident vigilance.

528 darkness

If you are surrounded by darkness, you
may experience hardship and a period
of confusion until daylight returns.

529 light

Light refers to consciousness and
self-knowledge. Daylight promises new
hope and fresh insights. A beam of light
signifies the answer to an old problem.

530 fire

Dreams of fire can signify
transformation, purification,
spiritual growth, love, anger,
destruction, or new beginnings.

531 ashes

Ashes and dust are often linked to the loss of a
person or object of great significance in your life,
coming to terms with an intense emotional
experience, or the need for atonement.

532 planets

To dream of visiting other planets
implies that you will soon enjoy
new and thrilling experiences.

533 moon

Seeing the moon in your dream suggests
death and rebirth; you may have to
surrender something to recover something
else of value. The moon also indicates
returning warmth after coldness.

To dream of Venus, the hottest planet, suggests that your love life will be tempestuous and full of incident.

535 Mercury

To dream of Mercury suggests that your activities will be imbued with power and that you will be an inspiration to others.

536 Earth

Dreaming of the planet Earth is a symbol of stability; it is time to attend to domestic matters.

To dream of Mars implies that you could find yourself in a power struggle that will require calm detachment and sound judgment if you are to prevail.

538 Jupiter

Seeing the gas giant Jupiter in your dreams suggests that you cannot stop what you have already set in motion.

539 Saturn

To dream of the ringed planet Saturn denotes a betrothal or a wedding; it also indicates shared experience and mutual support.

540 Neptune

The stormy blue planet Neptune appears serene when viewed from a distance; it is a sign of your ability to remain outwardly calm.

541 Uranus

The planet Uranus takes eighty-four years to orbit the sun; if it appears in your dream, it represents dedicated practice and planning. You may receive news from afar.

542 Pluto

The coldest planet in the solar system, Pluto suggests frozen beauty, loneliness, and the ceasing of all activity.

543 rocket

To dream of a rocket symbolizes explosive activity to overcome an obstacle or escape restrictive conditions; it also indicates the breaking of a contract.

544 sleigh

To dream of a sleigh relates to ease of movement and indifference to unfriendly criticism; you will eventually win a struggle with cunning competitors.

545 knots

When knots feature in a dream, they frequently bring protection and romantic stability; if you untie a knot, it may mean that you wish to dissolve a union or open yourself up in order to overcome a problem.

In a dream, oil or gasoline suggests that a combustible situation will cause turbulence in your domestic sphere; guide your emotional energies into constructive channels.

If a rope features in your dream, it symbolizes connections and responsibilities; you may be experiencing a conflict between family and career.

An anchor is a symbol of stability and security; if it appears in your dream, it indicates your need to define your boundaries and examine the routines that shape your waking life.

bow and arrow

A bow and arrow represent war and power; this may be a call for compassion as much as a symbolic call to arms.

550 rosette

Wearing a rosette implies that you will be showered with praise and prestigious accolades; your reputation will give you access to new areas of influence.

551 medals

To dream of wearing medals implies your desire for personal recognition; it may also express your need to find validation without relying on the opinions of others.

552 trophy

To dream of a trophy is a warning to avoid believing the voices of flattery; do not overextend yourself as a result of the confidence of previous successes.

553   female warrior

Dreaming of a female warrior indicates emancipation; you will overcome the prejudice of others by your extraordinary abilities.

554   flag

A flag can be a sign of conquest, submission, or group identity; this dream invites you to examine your goals in relation to a community or ideology.

555   handcuffs

To dream of handcuffs corresponds to feelings of powerlessness and to possible self-sabotage; others will judge you on your own terms.

An ax can be a symbol of destruction as well as of strenuous work; it invites you to reconsider a business relationship or your commitment to a project.

557 horseshoe

A horseshoe represents good luck and protection against misfortune; conditions are ripe for action in business.

558 envelope

An envelope represents the concealed power of the written word; do not be afraid to explore your thoughts and feelings in writing.

559 walking stick

A walking stick represents difficult progress and unpleasant tasks; to use one in a dream indicates fragile feelings and uncertain speculation.

560 package

To receive a package in your dream reveals an accepting, open nature; it also denotes improvement in health and energy.

bell

The sound of a bell in
your dream invites you to consider
your core values; when you are called
to account in your waking life, you
will prove your worth.

562 triangle

A triangle signifies deceit in your love life and might foretell separation from friends and a disruption of the status quo.

563 concert

Attending a concert in your dream denotes productive leisure and the company of urbane associates; also you may gain a new insight into an old problem by focusing your attention elsewhere.

564 choir

Dreaming of a choir indicates that productive teamwork will result in a flattering honor being bestowed upon you; take care to acknowledge the contribution of your companions.

A flute is associated with angels and enchantment; playing or hearing this instrument is a call for greater simplicity and inner resolve.

566   piano

To play the piano in your dream points to finding your place in society and striving for what you are naturally capable of becoming; it also refers to your contribution to your community.

567   oboe

An oboe denotes a favorable turn in conditions; you need not worry about lack of recognition as long as you act with modesty and openness.

568 tambourine

A tambourine suggests lavish extravagance and reckless behavior; it may be time to simplify your life.

569 trombone

To play or hear the trombone in your dream indicates that planning will bring fortunate results to an important enterprise and a realization of your wishes.

570 harp

Playing the harp in a dream denotes a rise to positions beyond your expectations; your reputation will be in jeopardy only if your self-discipline slips.

If you hear cymbals in your dream, it indicates that a personal crisis will soon reach its conclusion; the repercussions of previous decisions will now rise to prominence.

572 violin

To dream of a violin suggests a quarrelsome relationship and separation from family and friends; you will be called on to defend something that cannot be neglected.

573 clarinet

Dreaming of a clarinet suggests that uncertainty about the outcome of a project is making you anxious and suspicious; remember that certain undertakings need expert guidance.

574 trumpet

To hear or play a trumpet indicates that a time of judgment is approaching; trust the preparations that you have already made and avoid making strident remarks.

575 guitar

A guitar equates to a talent that is gradually fading away through neglect or a misguided belief that you should be doing something more productive; play to your strengths and interests.

576 spectacles

Dreaming of spectacles indicates that you will gain fresh insights concerning a familiar situation.

577 handkerchief

A handkerchief is a symbol of clandestine encounters and romantic intrigue.

578 purse

An empty purse is a symbol of bereavement and provokes an awareness of your own mortality.

579 ribbon

A ribbon often corresponds to a legal matter that demands immediate action; it may also draw attention to an obligation you will take on willingly.

580 disguise

To dream of being in disguise signifies the improvement of skills and the broadening of your abilities through unconventional means; you may enjoy a productive association with a stranger.

581 crown

A crown represents the elevation of the spirit above the body, but is also linked to unfaithfulness; suspicion and mistrust are obstructing your commitment.

582 ring

A ring, which has neither a beginning nor an end, denotes fidelity and eternity; if the ring is damaged then a contract will soon be broken.

583 match

If you strike a match in your dream, it denotes leadership qualities and the overcoming of adversities; if the match fails to light, you will be challenged by those who seek to undermine your authority.

584 smoking a pipe

If someone in your dream is smoking a pipe, it corresponds to a narrow escape from injury and the designs of enemies.

585   anniversary

To dream of an anniversary suggests your desire to balance old and new; it may also be calling you to appreciate great progress.

586   luggage

If luggage weighs you down and hinders your progress in a dream, it is a sign that an emotional issue is unresolved; if the lock on your luggage breaks then you will find the courage to confront your fears.

587 bubbles

Blowing bubbles represents unrealistic aspirations; vanity may be blinding you to your real areas of strength.

588 merry-go-round

If you are riding a merry-go-round, you are experiencing a period of stagnation in your life; your inability to welcome change may be preventing you from growing.

589 marbles

To dream of marbles relates to your observation and perception; your powers of reasoning will rescue you from a difficult position.

590 toys

Toys represent family enjoyment. If you give away toys, you seek the approval of others, and broken toys may mean that family relationships are long overdue for patching up.

591 dice

To see dice in a dream represents sudden change without warning; it also highlights the need to distinguish between value and worthlessness.

592 birthday

Dreaming of a birthday suggests impatience at the speed at which a project or undertaking is progressing; beware of focusing on the rewards rather than confronting obstacles.

593 ball

A dream that features a ball is connected to childhood and also to parental responsibility. Catching a ball represents a feeling of connection with your past; dropping a ball indicates feelings of not belonging.

594 television

To dream of watching television implies passive resistance to an unwanted influence; it may also allude to feelings of frustration with regard to career and aspirations.

595 book

A book is a symbol of wisdom and destiny. If you are writing in a book, you will be proactive; if you read a book, you will bide your time and acquire knowledge.

596 tweezers

Using tweezers in your dream corresponds to your attention to detail; if you become too pedantic, you risk ignoring the larger picture and losing sight of your major goals.

597 splinter

A splinter is a sign that you are allowing petty irritations to get under your skin; restore balance by establishing higher standards.

598 coins

Coins indicate that worldly attachment will cause conflict with a small act of kindness; giving money away is auspicious and signifies unexpected gains.

599 bucket

A bucket or pitcher represents overflowing abundance and long life.

600 hook

If you see a hook in your dream, it suggests that you are being drawn to something outside your normal sphere of activity; explore with confidence and use your intuition to avoid possible dangers.

601 anvil

When an anvil features in your dream it may mean you have been approaching a problem with too much force and should employ a more subtle solution.

602 knife

A knife may appear in your dream to indicate that something has been cut out of your sphere of influence; to wield a knife indicates feelings of powerlessness in your waking life.

603 scissors

A pair of scissors is linked to your destiny and the need to create opportunities rather than waiting for them to drop in your lap.

604 razor

If you dream of a razor, it denotes disagreements leading to the termination of an unhappy union; it also signifies betterment and personal gain.

605 machinery

If machinery features in your dream, it represents a conflict between your autonomy and the opinions and prejudices of those around you; you may encounter a situation where you must hide your true feelings to keep the peace.

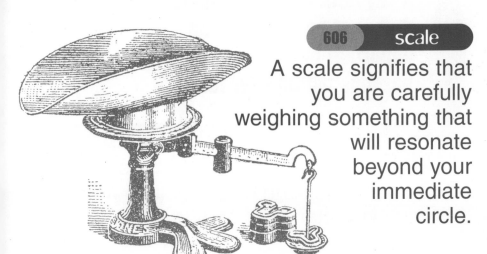

606 scale

A scale signifies that you are carefully weighing something that will resonate beyond your immediate circle.

607 locked door

A closed or locked door represents a missed opportunity or a regret. An open door denotes the realization of your wishes. Two or more doors represent choices, and a revolving door signifies stagnation.

608 key

A key both locks and unlocks; to dream of one denotes an important initiation or rite of passage within your family.

609 hourglass

An hourglass reminds you of the fleeting nature of time and the importance of seizing the moment.

610 open window

An open window implies easy success. A dirty window means you need to be more specific about a goal. Cleaning a window suggests persisting despite an obstacle or setback.

611 bath

Taking a bath or shower expresses your wish to purge your mind of unwanted thoughts; it also represents a fresh start or making a clean break.

612 towel

To use a towel in a dream suggests that you are anticipating a visitor; to drop a towel reveals that you are unprepared for an unexpected guest.

613 faucet

To dream of a faucet denotes abundant resources and opportunities for growth; if water flows from the faucet, you will enjoy recognition of your talents and the admiration of peers.

614 drain

A drain suggests stagnation and decay; you may be wasting your resources because of carelessness or procrastination.

615 chair

A chair represents how you see your place in life. A comfortable chair indicates contentment; an uncomfortable chair suggests you have much that you still wish to achieve.

616 table

A table is a symbol of community gathering and sustenance; appreciate your current blessings and look to your family for companionship.

617 clock

If you see a clock in your dream, it is often a sign that an important event or deadline is troubling you.

618 attic

Entering an attic represents a part of yourself that has been neglected or deliberately forgotten; an important issue demands your full attention and should not be ignored any longer.

619 basket

A basket appears in your dream as a symbol of fertility and maternal fulfillment; if the basket is full, new responsibilities and pleasures will ensue.

620 mousetrap

If a mousetrap features in your dream, it denotes impending danger; beware of being backed into a corner by unscrupulous business associates.

621 cobwebs

Cobwebs are associated with healing and perseverance; if you are nursing a grievance your fortitude will help you overcome any difficulties.

622 cave

A cave is a symbol of your unconscious mind and the unexplored parts of your psyche; it can be a place either of refuge or of self-exploration.

623 bellows

Bellows represent the relationship between the body and the spirit; they highlight the importance of your mental and physical health.

624 rust

If you see rust in your dream, it represents an area of your waking life that is stagnant or unrewarding.

**If you see a fountain
in your dream, it suggests access to
hidden resources and a strong intention
expressed completely.**

Action
Dreams

626 flying

A dream about flying indicates a momentary release from a stressful situation; it is usually accompanied by a recognition that responsibilities cannot be ignored for very long.

627 ballooning

To ride in a balloon is a thrilling and breathtaking experience; if the balloon drifts away, it may mean that you are exposing yourself to unnecessary risks. A calm ride represents healthy growth in all areas of your life.

628 skiing

Skiing suggests that a project that is gaining momentum requires your immediate and diligent attention.

Flying a kite in a dream alludes to your ability to bring a childlike sense of fun to your business dealings; know, enjoy, and believe in what you are doing.

630 rowing

Rowing is an ambiguous image that involves moving forward while facing backward; a project or relationship may be headed in the right direction even though logic tells you otherwise.

631 surfing

Surfing connotes spontaneous, overflowing, and unrestrained joy; abandon posturing in favor of an honest expression of your true feelings.

632 canoeing

Canoeing stands for adventure and physical triumph; it also indicates a refusal to be restricted by others' boundaries or lack of vision.

633 swimming

Swimming is usually an indication of success; if you are sinking or drowning, it means that you feel overwhelmed by your responsibilities. Diving into water refers to an escape from a potentially embarrassing situation.

634 fishing

To dream of fishing expresses a need to prove yourself worthy of the trust that has been placed in you by important companions.

635 running

Running reveals a strong desire to shine above your peers. Difficulty running is a sign that you are sabotaging your own chances of success.

636 climbing

Climbing to the top of a mountain shows that you will overcome whatever hinders your quest for excellence; failure to reach the top may indicate that you are climbing the wrong mountain.

637 baseball

Playing baseball suggests single-minded purposefulness combined with the desire to be a good team player.

638 golf

Playing golf relates to your pursuit of an ideal; if you play badly, your idealism may be hampering your efficiency.

639 football

Playing football represents gathering together for mutual gain; a situation will arise that will allow you to demonstrate your trust and team spirit.

640 bowling

To bowl denotes the dividing up of belongings, or the settling of an old score; a struggle over precious possessions will cause distress.

641 skating

Skating implies that
a project that appears to be
running smoothly may contain
hidden risks.

To dream of cricket implies that long periods of inactivity will contain moments where decisive action will affect the final outcome.

643 table tennis

Table tennis equates to attaining order and harmony through attention to detail and the application of formal rules.

644 wrestling

Wrestling in a dream corresponds to inner turmoil both physical and mental; temperance and moderation will restore your balance and make you feel more positive.

645 hockey

Playing hockey denotes confrontation between two opinions; conflict may be avoided by consistent behavior that builds trust slowly.

646 hunting

Hunting suggests your need to exert excessive control over your environment; a more relaxed approach will bring you greater happiness.

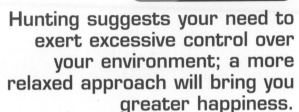

647 trampoline

A trampoline represents physical and mental confidence and indicates your willingness to enjoy new challenges and experiences.

648 gymnastics

Gymnastics corresponds to feelings of physical inadequacy and may be a sign of mental or emotional stress.

649 hay gathering

If you gather hay in your dream, you risk failing to reap the full benefits of an investment through negligence or greed.

650 ditch

If you climb out of a ditch in your dream you may regain your health and renew your vitality; even falling down a ditch may suggest a blessing in disguise.

bicycle riding

To dream of riding a bicycle shows confidence in your own abilities; if you are racing downhill you may be missing the view in favor of hastily chasing your goals.

652 chopping

Chopping a tree or logs suggests that you
may be required to confront a personal
issue in order to resolve an awkward
relationship that is making you restless.

Carving on a tree signifies divination and interpretation; you will advance through conscious awareness and foresight.

654 mowing

Mowing a lawn means that your social commitments and duties are becoming a burden; if the lawn is dry, you should think about yourself more, rather than pleasing others.

655 gardening

Gardening implies skillful financial management and patient planning; you will enjoy unprecedented returns on a shrewd investment.

Playing cards indicates that your future is less certain than you had previously thought; a tactical maneuver will be necessary to help you achieve your objectives.

657 photograph

Taking a photograph in your dream suggests that you wish to hold power over someone in your waking life.

658 chess

Playing chess highlights the importance of logical planning for the purpose of gaining advantage in a dispute; strategic withdrawal may be a sign of personal strength.

659 conducting

If you find yourself conducting an orchestra, you will exercise great power; be mindful of the rights of others.

660   dancing

A dream in which you are dancing is an invitation to approach your waking life with more enjoyment and sometimes a sense of disciplined fun.

661 meditating

Meditating in a dream suggests that to find meaning you should lead a simple life in harmony with nature.

662 yoga

Performing yoga in a dream suggests a need to gain control over your physical and mental energies; it also indicates a need to be governed by what you do and not what you think and believe.

663 painting

Painting in a dream denotes change toward completion that takes place at the proper time. Remember that everything proceeds at its own pace.

664 auction

Taking part in an auction warns of a dangerous situation; your desire to win may cause you to overextend yourself or make a rash decision.

665 obstacles

To jump successfully over obstacles indicates that you view your problems as opportunities. If you hurt yourself or fall over, you need to rethink your strategy.

Jumping over a low wall points to focused progress in your business affairs; if you jump a high wall, you will enjoy taking unnecessary risks.

667 airplane

Traveling by airplane expresses both a desire for adventure and the need to place your trust in others to reach new horizons.

668 driving

Driving a vehicle usually refers to the way in which you direct and manage your waking life; the way in which you drive highlights important facets of your personality and your self-image.

669 taxi

Dreaming of riding in a taxi brings good luck and suggests that you should sit back and trust another to guide you to your destination.

670 escalator

To ride an escalator suggests that you will reach your goals with ease; be especially vigilant at the beginning and end of a project.

To dream of sleeping indicates that you are ignoring or escaping from a situation that requires your patient attention; now is the time to face your responsibilities to loved ones or business colleagues.

672 chopping food

Chopping food denotes the anticipation of pleasant company and shared enjoyment.

673 cooking

Cooking in a dream implies that you should focus your creativity on providing emotional nourishment for those around you; do not leave your work in the care of others.

674 shopping

Visiting stores relates to your material aspirations; if you make a purchase, you can expect prosperity and good fortune.

675 bus

When you dream of riding on a bus, you are experiencing frustration at the pace of your progress; it is time to acknowledge that other people are a blessing and not a hindrance.

676 cable car

Riding in a cable car indicates that a thrilling opportunity will take you into unfamiliar territory from which you will return with difficulty or reluctance.

If you miss your train in a dream or are traveling on the wrong train, it means you have chosen the wrong path or are trying to do too many things at once.

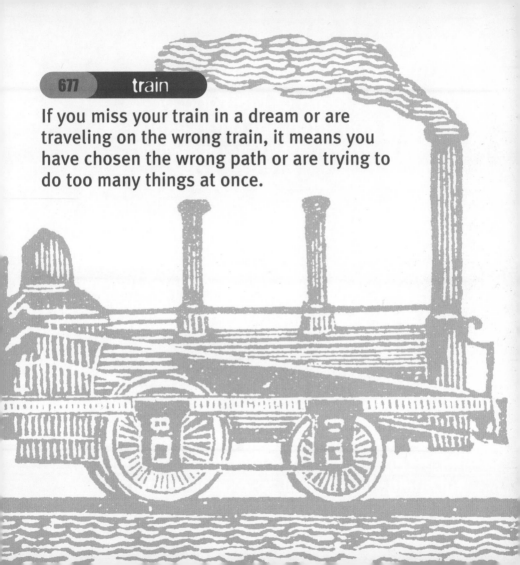

678 breaking/mending

When you dream of breaking or mending something, it often expresses a need to resolve a difficulty within a relationship.

679 crawling

To dream of crawling indicates that you will make slow progress and may undergo unpleasant tasks to reach your goals.

680 chasing

If you chase someone in a dream, it is important to discover what you are really pursuing; it is a call to examine your goals and strategies for achieving them.

681 sliding

To dream of sliding denotes that a business venture is running away with you; alternatively it may be a warning that things are not running as smoothly as they might seem.

682 praying

To pray in a dream is to seek support for a problem that seems beyond your powers; approach the matter with self-belief and commitment, and you will succeed.

683 magic

Dreaming that you can perform magic indicates that your imagination and creative powers will help you achieve wonders; carry this empowering feeling into your waking life rather than regret the moment when you wake up.

684 throwing

Throwing something in a dream may represent a need to acquire the thing that is being thrown; a target is often the focus of negative feelings such as envy or anger.

685 digging

Digging a hole relates to negative thinking that is frustrating your efforts; filling a hole with soil or water shows a willingness to let go of past wrongs.

686 shoveling

Shoveling snow or dirt suggests a need for increased dedication to win over the hearts of colleagues; move forward one step at a time.

687 sweating

Sweating in a dream suggests that although hard work is uncomfortable at the moment, you will soon reap the benefit of your endeavors.

688 kneeling

Kneeling down represents humility or subordination; when you ascend to new levels of influence, do not lose sight of the ground below.

689 swinging

Swinging in a dream represents the ebb and flow of natural growth; as well as the inner peace that comes with being carried along in a natural and unforced way.

690 stumble

When you stumble or trip in your dream, it may mean that you will take the first step to solving a problem by acknowledging its existence; also remember that a mistake is the best learning experience.

691 walking

Dreaming of walking through a swamp expresses a loss of confidence in friendships and disorder within the family.

692 puddle

To step in a puddle denotes peace and good fortune; it is also connected to your aspirations, because by looking in a puddle you may view a small portion of the sky.

693 wading

Wading through water signifies progress in the face of adversity; wading through mud denotes a loss of self-esteem through what you perceive as your own incompetence.

To walk or run barefoot indicates a sense of freedom; if your feet are painful, you are being overambitious or reckless in some area of your life.

695 limping

Limping denotes your determination to overcome any obstacle; if you fall over, you can expect sympathy from an unexpected direction.

696 skipping

Skipping suggests that you will negotiate obstacles with ease and lightness of touch; it also refers to repeated emotions and learning self-mastery.

697 selling

If you sell something in a dream, you may be the first to spot an opportunity that others have overlooked; do not ignore an idea just because it seems obvious.

698 getting water

Getting water signifies instruction and enlightenment; you will find what you are searching for only if you are prepared to share it with others.

699 baby carriage

To push a baby carriage indicates your preoccupation with family relationships; you may need to enforce legitimate demands in a delicate domestic situation.

700 shivering

Shivering in a dream hints at an involuntary reaction to a frosty reception; your body language may betray you in a delicate situation.

701 sneeze

If you sneeze in a dream, it is likely that you will receive a gift before the end of the week; sneezing is also connected to truthfulness and someone speaking highly of you.

702 spitting

Spitting is frequently associated with good luck; it also relates to the sealing of a contract and offers protection against the forces of nature.

703 whistling

Whistling in a dream is unlucky; to see someone else whistling indicates that you are being misinformed in order to protect your feelings.

704 winking

Winking in a dream denotes laughter and a faithful romantic relationship; your partner may be planning a surprise gathering in your name.

705 clapping

Clapping expresses your own need for praise and approval; do not seek the affirmation of others as a solution to every problem.

Shaking hands with someone indicates success in financial matters or that it is time to forgive someone who has wronged you.

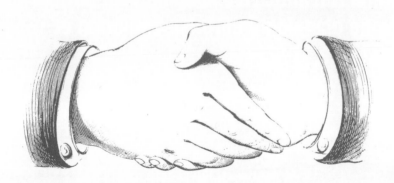

If you hide in your dream, it implies that you risk glossing over your achievements and turning away from your potential; remember that striving is not always linked to vanity.

708 hanging upside down

To hang upside down indicates that you are open to new and unusual ways of seeing the world; expect a change of perspective to bring magical rewards.

709 walking under a ladder

Walking under a ladder indicates that you are not moving in harmony with the prevailing currents.

Carrying something relates to your ability to handle a physical or mental challenge in your waking life.

711 waving

To dream of waving means you are capable of forming productive associations; it also highlights the importance of fostering the development of those around you.

712 standing in line

To stand in a line represents the relationship between personal free will and the constraints of circumstances; if you wait your turn, you will gain greater benefits.

713 deliver

If you deliver something in a dream, it is usually linked to your attitude toward your professional skills and your ability to reach certain targets.

714   kissing

Kissing suggests a pleasant romantic liaison or reciprocation from the object of your affections.

715   stirring

Stirring corresponds to your ability to capitalize on existing resources and to your imaginative use of current circumstances.

716   hopping

To dream of hopping suggests that a self-imposed obstacle may be blocking your progress.

Coughing represents restlessness arising from the failure to exploit your full potential.

Spinning around is related to intense activity taking you nowhere; you will not make progress until you identify repeated mistakes and begin to learn from them.

Itching indicates that a niggling worry that you have not addressed will grow bigger unless you confront it decisively.

720 storytelling

Storytelling in a dream highlights energies
originating in the past that are still active in
the present; draw strength by looking back.

721 hypnotize

If someone tries to hypnotize you in a
dream, it indicates your need for
learning through receptive relaxation; it
also signifies the turning of potential
into physical reality.

722 cigarettes

To dream of cigarettes indicates that
someone else will exploit you at a time
of need; do not undertake anything
while in a nervous frame of mind.

723 writing

Writing relates to creating your own story and life path; you may need to analyze your aspirations to find a clearer direction.

724 sending a letter

Sending a letter indicates that you may make contact with an old friend; do not allow your competitive nature to sour a reunion.

725 text messages

Sending text messages indicates a network of friendships and the promise of romantic intrigue; a secret admirer will reveal his or her feelings soon.

726 pushing

Pushing corresponds to your attitude toward what you seek to gain by manipulating others; ask yourself whether you are pushing with the correct amount of force.

727 pulling

Pulling something in a dream symbolizes your attitude to a close relationship; you risk alienating a close friend by your overdependence or need for approval.

728 exercise

If you dream that you are exercising vigorously you need to consider whether you should be leading a more energetic life.

729 prize

Winning a prize may mean that an
incident that you have treated as a
misfortune will eventually lead to
unexpected benefits.

730 money

Counting money in a dream symbolizes
insecurity about financial commitments;
you may be prioritizing income
over expenditure.

731 lend

To lend something in a dream shows generosity of spirit and advancement through empathy and ungrudging conduct.

732 stealing

To dream of stealing equates to your desire to rob someone of the recognition that they deserve; jealousy and frustration may be paralyzing your concentration and your will.

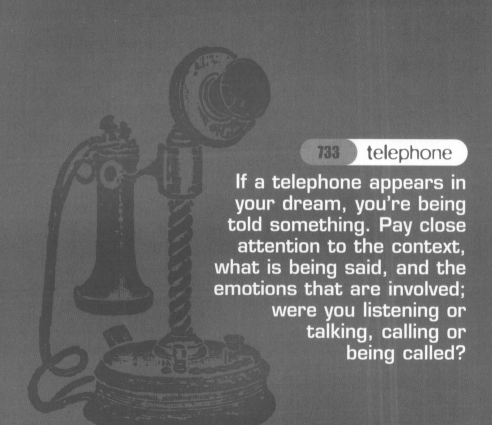

733 telephone

If a telephone appears in your dream, you're being told something. Pay close attention to the context, what is being said, and the emotions that are involved; were you listening or talking, calling or being called?

734 working

Dreams about working or studying are classic anxiety dreams and mean it's time to calm down and relax a bit more.

735 typing

Typing or keying in a dream denotes advancement through established routines or methods.

736 operating machinery

To dream of operating machinery signifies a mechanistic attitude toward a friendship in which you may be lacking empathy.

737 combing your hair

To dream of combing or washing your hair points toward anxiety at the approach of an important meeting or event.

738 shaving

Shaving a part of your body foretells mastery of your affairs; someone else shaving you reveals your concern about being taken advantage of or defrauded.

739 washing

Washing any part of your body denotes that you are trying to put the past behind you to bring your plans to fruition.

740 building

Building corresponds to great strength and creativity; you will accomplish a project with confidence and dexterity.

741 saw

Using a saw in your dream corresponds to your desire to take on responsibility for something that should be left to nature; listen to advice and examine your motives.

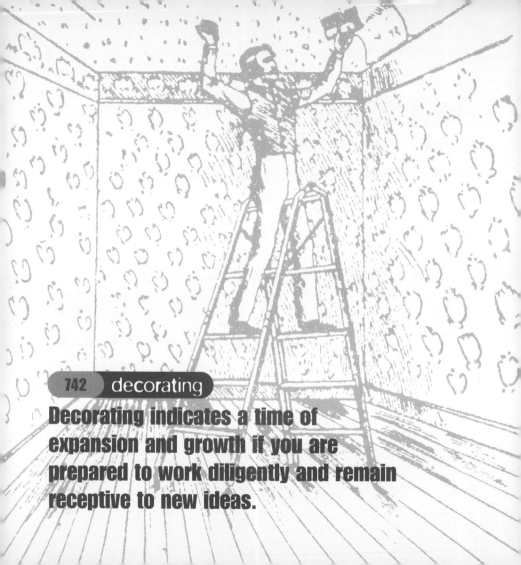

742 decorating

Decorating indicates a time of expansion and growth if you are prepared to work diligently and remain receptive to new ideas.

743 hammer

Using a hammer in a dream denotes power, strength, and protection, but it is also a symbol of binding transaction; substantive communication will aid your business ventures.

744 drilling

If you dream of drilling, it indicates that you are willing to drive a course through all obstructions to progress; it also refers to concentration of the mind.

745 new residence

To change your residence suggests that you should establish new contacts and avoid risky situations; it also encourages you to embrace change and maintain a clear vision at all times.

746 knitting

A dream of knitting, sewing, or weaving may be a call to broaden your horizons.

747 vacuum cleaner

Using a vacuum cleaner relates to issues of control in your waking life and often accompanies feelings of powerlessness and anxiety.

748 ironing

Ironing suggests that your attempts to straighten out a recent misunderstanding will yield satisfactory results.

mending clothes

Mending clothes can be a sign that you are making the best of a difficult situation, but it may symbolize unnecessary thrift.

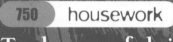

750 housework

To dream of doing housework is usually a sign that something in your waking life is causing you anxiety; clearing your mental clutter will help you think with greater clarity.

Magic, Mysteries and the Metaphysical

751 magic

Magic means a pleasant surprise awaits you, or it can be a sign that you are seeking the easy way out of a difficult situation.

752 invisibility

Invisibility in a dream can feel very empowering, but it may also highlight feelings of insignificance and of being overlooked.

753 spell

To dream of being under a spell implies that you may succumb to temptations that you feel powerless to resist. It is time to consider the consequences of your actions.

754 witch

Dreaming of a witch represents being faced with a difficult choice; you will experience moral ambivalence, rather than simply being able to follow your conscience.

755 wizard

A wizard indicates that you may be trying to solve a problem by trusting luck rather than by planning; good things do not always come to those who wait.

756 fairy

A fairy is always a favorable sign, showing that you have an open heart and a trusting nature.

757 magic wand

Using a magic wand in your dream suggests that you will use deception to obtain your wishes; if someone else uses a wand, you may be unknowingly serving the designs of a deceitful person.

758 centaur

Half man, half horse, the mythical centaur appears in your dream to warn of confrontation in business; you risk losing close relations with powerful allies.

759 ghost

The ghost of a loved one implies that you are exposed to danger and need to trust the opinions of those who care deeply for you.

760 sphinx

With its lion's body, human face, and wings, the mythical sphinx is a benevolent creature that embodies royalty and suggests that your interests will be encouraged by those with influence.

343

761 poltergeist

A poltergeist corresponds to feelings that currently threaten to find expression in an unwanted outburst.

762 cyclops

In a dream, the giant one-eyed cyclops symbolizes a hasty union with someone who is unsuited to you; you need to be circumspect about romantic impulses.

763 minotaur

If you see a man with a bull's head, it is the mythical minotaur, which appears in your dream to highlight the need to limit yourself to a chosen field of action.

764 mermaid

In a dream, a mermaid denotes vision, mystery, and the power of unconscious desires. Expect a strange adventure involving romance and temptation.

765 banshee

If you see a haggard, wailing woman, it may be the mythical banshee, which appears in your dream to warn of sadness caused by death or dishonor.

766 halo

Seeing someone with a halo indicates your desire to emulate that person.

767 genie

If a genie or jinn appears in your dream, you may be relying on a powerful helper for your advancement; the value of this person may be judged only by the degree to which you retain your independence.

768 angels

Dreaming of angels corresponds to your search for a guiding influence, secular or spiritual; you must convince yourself with fundamental reasons of the suitability of a forthcoming project.

769 unicorn

A unicorn represents the triumph of the rational mind over your physical urges; you are experiencing a conflict between your mind and body.

770 griffin

To dream of a griffin signifies vigilant strength; you will bat your way through difficulties to overcome all resistance.

771 sea horse

Dreaming of a sea horse indicates role reversal and unusual creativity; peculiar responsibilities that at first seem incongruous will become familiar and enjoyable.

772 winged horse

A winged horse represents the freeing of the spirit from worldly bonds; harness your inner power to push forward a cherished undertaking.

773 behemoth

If you see a huge, heavy, unfamiliar beast, it may be the mythical behemoth; misfortune that cannot be avoided must be endured.

774 phoenix

Reborn from its own ashes, the mythical phoenix makes an appearance in your dream to reveal a reversal of your fortunes; a project that appeared doomed will soon prosper.

775   elf

An elf suggests that you
enjoy displaying your
wisdom; remember that the
conscious mind is a tool.

776   druid

If you see a druid in your dream, you
will enjoy long life; peace and truth will
accompany your actions.

777 scarab

The scarab beetle is a powerful protector; if you see it in a dream, you may enjoy a resolution of a family dispute.

778 snake

A small snake with a white crownlike marking on its head is the mythical basilisk, and dreaming of one is a warning about the presence of a petty tyrant and bad fortune.

779 dragon

If you dream of a
dragon, you may be
permitting yourself
to be ruled by your
passions and your
impulsiveness will
land you in hot water.

780 black cat

If a black cat appears in your dream,
it will bring you good luck. Now is the time
to give your vocation greater priority.

781 abominable snowman

The abominable snowman is a symbol of strength during a time of isolation and loneliness; it connotes triumph through single-minded courage and principled action.

782 Loch Ness monster

The Loch Ness monster represents disappointment as a result of questionable or superficial goals; it also indicates misunderstanding and separation in a close relationship.

chimera

With the head of a lion and the body of a goat, the mythical chimera appears in your dream to represent a conflict of interest between friends and family that will require skillful negotiation.

784 kelpie

Part horse and part bull, and with two sharp horns, the mythical Kelpie represents misfortune arising from hasty schemes for short-term gain; a rash business venture will attract trouble and lead to hardship.

785 faun

With the body of a deer and the face of a human, a faun appears in your dream to denote gentle mischief; you may be the unwitting target of a practical joke or prankster.

786 anka

If you dream of a huge bird, it may be the mythical Arabian anka, which highlights the need to resist provocation from disruptive influences; sometimes a show of strength is more effective than quiet diplomacy.

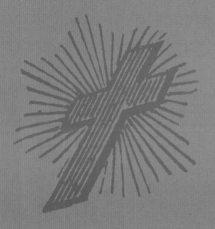

787 crucifix

A crucifix points to the inner strength that you will need to draw upon to see you through a crisis. Kissing a cross implies resignation to a misfortune.

788 crucifixion

A dream involving crucifixion points to an extremely difficult or painful trial in your waking life.

To dream of a hassock represents meekness or modesty in behavior; you may be obliged to show deferential respect to a person of high position.

790   temple

A temple indicates your desire for spiritual guidance; it is time to acknowledge the divisiveness of wealth.

791 celebration

Participating in a religious celebration in a dream is an invitation to enjoy the beauty of creation and human fellowship, and to be released from need.

792 conflict

To dream of religious conflict is a reminder of the untrusting side of human nature; a one-sided view of the world will bring only unhappiness.

793 sacrifice

If you witness or participate in an animal sacrifice in a dream, it may mean that you are turning someone into a scapegoat.

794 baptism of a child

Viewing the baptism of a child in a dream indicates an awareness of the need to reestablish family connections.

795 baptism of self

To be baptized yourself suggests the death of old ways and being reborn; it promises good luck and renewed vitality.

A dream about nuns signifies a need for active service or devotion; you will gain the opportunity to reassess your lifestyle with a view to achieving spiritual independence.

797   Allah, Buddha, Christ

To dream of Allah, Buddha, or Christ corresponds to your desire to open yourself spiritually; if you have recently been neglecting this aspect of your life, now is the time to make it a top priority.

798   crypt

Visiting a crypt in a dream alludes to morbid feelings of self-doubt that are holding you back; a new project will bring increased self-esteem.

799 holy water

If holy water features in your dream, you will be protected against the scurrilous attacks of your enemies by the support of noble and influential friends.

800 icon

If a religious icon makes an appearance in your dream it may signify that you have distanced yourself from authentic spirituality by being overly concerned with the trappings.

801 stigmata

Experiencing stigmata in your dream corresponds to your feelings about religious ecstasy or hysteria and invites you to examine unresolved spiritual issues.

802 prayer beads

Prayer beads relate to inner truth, your search for spiritual fulfillment, and the resolution of a personal doctrinal conflict.

803 altar

An altar indicates that you must make a sacrifice to remain true to your inner spirit; it also represents protection and sanctuary.

804 gargoyle

A gargoyle signifies that you will be the last to catch on to a situation that appears obvious to those around you.

805 vestments

To wear liturgical vestments denotes a desire to demonstrate more fully the outward expression of your inner spirituality.

806 pulpit

A pulpit represents your need for atonement through religious observance; if you stand in a pulpit, it suggests the postponement of material desires.

monks

To dream of monks
suggests being
united for a common
purpose; it may
indicate a desire to
be more active
within your family or
community.

A prayer rug evokes divine protection and religious devotion; it highlights the importance of sacred time and space in your waking life.

809 being asleep

To dream of being asleep often brings with it a feeling of powerlessness and anxiety. It suggests that you feel trapped in your personal or professional dealings.

810 chalice

To drink from a chalice in a dream indicates receptivity, psychic ability, and your intuitive powers; you will be unusually sensitive to the nuances present in all your interactions.

811 celestial music

If you hear celestial music in a dream, it highlights your ability to enjoy something purely for its own sake.

Smelling or seeing incense burning represents your prayers rising to heaven; loved ones need to feel that they can count on your permanent support.

813 skull

The appearance of a skull denotes unpropitious change; your personal interests will cause you to seek association with strangers who will bring disagreeable obstructions.

A pentagram is a powerful symbol of protection and safety; if you dream of one, it means that when you set out on a risky venture, you will enjoy a rapid rise to distinction.

If a coffin features in your dream, take careful note of its appearance, because it is likely to contain a symbolic representation of the physical world that surrounds you.

816   devil

To dream of a devil relates to disturbing feelings of guilt that are threatening to destroy a close relationship; it may highlight a disruption within the family.

817 pleasant voices

Hearing pleasant voices is an indicator of fruitful reconciliation; if the voices are distressed or angry, you are feeling guilty about a relationship.

818 whispering voices

Whispering voices are a warning that you will be affected by the gossiping of false friends. Have confidence in your own abilities and hold your head high.

819 amulet

To dream of an amulet
brings good luck and protection
against the powers of fate; also
self-determination and courage.

820 divining rod

A divining rod represents things
that are hidden; you will find
disappointments where success
and pleasure seemed to await you.

821 rock carvings

Rock carvings symbolize eternal renewal through language and creative expression; they also represent enhanced memory and speech.

822 hexagram

A hexagram suggests the coming together of opposites; you will be roused to action by someone whom you have until now considered an antagonist or opponent.

A pyramid represents hierarchical structures and power struggles; business matters may be turbulent when they clash with your ambitious desires.

824 monolith

A monolith represents immovability or uniformity; you will face a difficult choice concerning your affiliation to a group or organization.

376

825 runes

Dreaming of runes indicates that a
cherished possession will take on a
mysterious significance; you may receive
an unusual gift from a loved one.

826 sundial

If a sundial features in your dream, it means you
must seek out those who are keen to accept
what you have to offer; make a point of
recognizing the wisdom of others.

827 pendulum

A pendulum suggests that you are
swinging back and forth from one opinion
to another; delaying a choice will cause
only confusion and hardship.

377

828 candlestick

A seven-branched candlestick represents the seven days of creation; divine order will help you stand firm no matter how difficult conditions become.

829 scroll

A scroll suggests the creative power of the word and the ability of human consciousness to rearrange base materials into an ordered form.

830 shaman

Seeing a shaman suggests that the unseen will be revealed to you; the ungraspable and the unknown is close at hand.

A chariot symbolizes an inexorable process against which you can do nothing; a certain sequence of events may be under way that is out of your control.

To dream of a shield indicates that you need to retreat to an area of safety in order to reassess your present position and claim what is rightfully yours.

A broken mirror is a symbol of bad luck arising through distorted self-perception; in your waking life you may face a challenging reappraisal of your strengths and weaknesses.

834 sword

To handle a sword in your dream indicates that you will take decisive action to end a period of doubt.

835 hieroglyphics

To see strange letters such as hieroglyphic symbols indicates that it is necessary to make careful plans to prepare for a drastic change.

836 riddle

Dreaming of a riddle implies that truth is being revealed to you in an oblique manner; concentrate on the connections that exist below the surface of things to see the world in a fresh way.

837 oracle

An oracle denotes new insights; you will take significant steps toward overcoming an imbalance.

838 maypole

If a maypole (which is representative of the rowan tree) plays a part in your dream, it suggests powerful protection, shared experience, and mutual support.

839 trident

When a trident appears in your dream, you will receive protection during a journey over water.

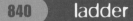
840 ladder

A ladder is an aspirational symbol of ascent or spiritual initiation; if you feel threatened from all sides, keep moving toward your goal and you will rise above your antagonists.

841 staircase

Like the ladder, a staircase is a symbol of spiritual development; a spiral staircase represents constant renewal and the cultivation of inner qualities.

drum

If you bang a drum in a dream, you are calling other people's attention to you; if you hear a drum, it presages a storm or conflict in your household.

843 broom

A broom represents ritual and secular cleansing but is also associated with witchcraft; it highlights a conflict between diligent labor and quick fixes.

844 stone circle

A circle made with stones in your dream denotes a powerful energy field supporting your interests; now is a good time to seize opportunities.

845 charm bracelet

Wearing a charm bracelet indicates protection and the power of resistance, as well as the safeguarding of property.

A fireplace is connected to the realm of the spirits and in a dream encourages you to explore your intuitive and instinctive powers.

An empty rocking chair may mean that bad influences will enter your household through negligence or indifference; trust only those who have shown themselves to be trustworthy.

848 telepathy

The practice of telepathy in a dream denotes connection through exchange; it means that you are well placed to deepen a recently formed friendship.

849 psychokinesis

If you experience psychokinesis (the power to move or change objects) in a dream, it is an indication of your focused intention to carry a matter through to its conclusion.

850 psychometry

To read experiences, facts, or feelings from an object in a dream is called psychometry and is a reminder that your thoughts really do have the power to make things happen.

851 déjà vu

Déjà vu and recurring dreams are your subconscious trying to make you acknowledge something significant that you are blocking in your waking life; pay special attention to the content of these dreams.

force field

To dream of a force field indicates that you need to cure an imbalance in your body's energy; it also implies your need for protection and security.

853 past life

Visiting a past life in a dream refers to the natural conclusion of a process so that something new may be created. It's time to move on.

854 tarot cards

Dreaming of tarot cards reveals that you feel uncertain about the future; if you resist the easy options, you will soon feel more in control of your ambitions.

855   aura

If you see someone's aura in a dream, it is a sign of intangible qualities in others that you are currently overlooking and a need for greater subtlety in your close relationships.

856   ouija board

A Ouija board warns of misfortune arising from suggestibility and the emphasis upon fears rather than wishes.

857   crystal ball

A crystal ball suggests your eagerness to take the next step or push forward to a higher level.

858 candle

A candle is a symbol of strength and honesty; you will attract genuine friendships and inspire others when you act with sincerity and singleness of purpose.

859 fireworks

Fireworks suggest joy and good health; their exotic, magical nature signifies traveling or a passionate encounter.

860 spacecraft

A spacecraft suggests prosperity under hazardous conditions; if you run from danger, you will be threatened with losses and misfortune.

861 comet

If you see a comet in your dream, you will befriend a passionate and charismatic person who will awaken you to new possibilities in your career.

862 shooting star

A shooting star is a sign of the gratification of a desire.

863 amethyst

A dream of purple amethyst is associated with humility, sincerity, and peace of mind; it is also connected to an apology or admission of wrongdoing.

864 emeralds

In a dream, emeralds symbolize rebirth and enduring love; you will enjoy intelligence and the gift of eloquence.

865   moonstone

The moonstone—also known as the goddess stone—appears in your dream as a symbol of gentleness and compassion; it is also associated with female magical energy.

866   rubies

Rubies foretell dramatic romance, passion, and intense desire arising from a completely new direction; or you will encounter a paramour from your past.

867 amber

To dream of amber corresponds to a desire to serve humanity, but it is also associated with the intellect and sexual potency.

868 opal

If you dream of a multicolored and mystical opal, it suggests rapid transformation that brings only good fortune and happiness.

869 turquoise

A dream in which the gem turquoise appears is indicative of foresight and protection from danger; a fading turquoise gem indicates a lover's dishonesty.

Diamonds indicate inner purity and clear thinking that lead to good fortune and contentment; a financial matter will take a mysterious turn.

871 topaz

Topaz represents good fortune and longevity; you will be overwhelmed by unexpected profit.

872 jasper

Jasper indicates stable emotions and grounded reality; you may be approaching a calm and balanced phase in your waking life that will allow you to touch base with your core beliefs.

873 sapphires

Sapphires correspond to the healing of illness and despair; a time of hardship is coming to an end and the future holds magical surprises.

874 bloodstone

Bloodstone, the green gem flecked with red, suggests that curative powers surround and protect you from harm; it is also associated with courage amid suffering.

875 marble

A dream involving marble denotes enchanting love interest and an extraordinary encounter with an elegant individual; it also signifies passion concealed by a cool exterior.

Nightmares

**To dream of being locked out of or otherwise unable to find a way into your house indicates a profoundly unsettling upheaval that is making you feel disoriented and insecure;
it often marks the starting point for finding a solution.**

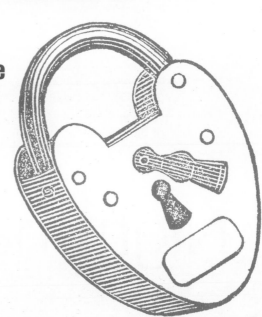

breaking a window

To dream of breaking a window indicates an imminent change in circumstances; if the breakage involves an injury, then the change will cause temporary hardship.

878 elevator

To dream of being stuck in an elevator relates to frustrated ambitions in business; maybe you need to be more proactive rather than waiting for things to change of their own accord.

inanimate object

An inanimate object coming to life and becoming a threat is related to your concerns about financial commitments.

880 dollar bills

To dream of dollar bills indicates low resources; at this time do not attempt to go beyond the bounds of what is possible.

881 mirror

Seeing a strange
reflection in a mirror
is connected with
your sense of
personal identity; it
often concerns
something you can
hide from others but
not from yourself.

882 ensnared

Dreaming of being ensnared indicates that your aspirations are being stifled and your abilities are not being recognized; you must champion your own unique qualities.

883 caught in a trap

If you are caught in a trap in a dream, it means you will be outsmarted by your opponents. You are being diverted from your goals by distractions and frivolity.

884 standing on the edge

To stand on the edge of a high place in a dream corresponds to a decision that can no longer be avoided; expect your feelings about jumping to be ambiguous, since most choices are rarely simple.

885 heights

A dream in which you are frightened by heights is an indication that a personal challenge is threatening your competence.

If your car won't start in a dream it may mean that you lack the courage or expertise to fix a problem.

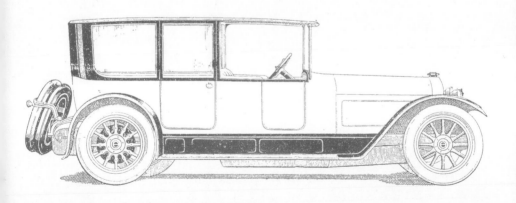

887 collision

To dream of a collision indicates that two or more conflicting forces are disrupting your thoughts; it may also suggest that there is more than one way of viewing a demanding problem.

888 losing control

To dream of losing control of a car may refer to recklessness or a shortsighted approach to the feelings of others.

889 traveling fast

Traveling uncomfortably fast corresponds to your impatience and risk taking; you should adopt a more gradual, progressive approach to avoid thoughtless blunders.

890 being lost

If you dream of becoming lost, you may be reluctant or unable to face the unknown; try to see an unfamiliar landscape as an opportunity rather than as a threat.

891 lost in a maze

Becoming lost in a maze or labyrinth suggests you may be protecting yourself against uncomfortable feelings of change by engaging in repetitive and mindless activities.

892 losing a race

Losing a race or challenge indicates the frustration of narrowly missing an opportunity; you must forgive yourself and remain alert to the chances that lie ahead.

893 lost in a forest

Getting lost in a forest relates to fears of parental separation or abandonment; it is also a sign that you should place more faith in your own ingenuity and resourcefulness.

894 tunnel

Crawling through or being trapped in a narrow tunnel is connected to anxiety about birth or death; you may also be blaming parents for something that is beyond their control.

895 something hanging

If you see something hanging above you that threatens to fall, it means you must act swiftly to avoid danger or confrontation; even if it falls and misses, you must still remain vigilant.

896 being unprepared

Dreaming of being unprepared for an important event such as an examination, making a speech, or performing in a play indicates that you are anxious about the preparations for a significant public event.

897 missing an exam

Missing an exam or important meeting is a common dream that expresses a reluctance to submit to rules and authority; it may also mean that you are placing improbable demands on yourself.

898 lost in a crowd

Being lost in a crowd highlights your need to stand out from the herd and raise your status.

899 open space

If, in a dream, you find yourself in an open space and feel frightened as a result, you may be anxious about lack of accomplishment and choice. If resources are diminished, do not put on an outward show, but ask for support.

900 searching

A dream about searching can often be frustrating and exhausting; it is usually a sign that you are lacking something in your waking life but have not yet consciously admitted it to yourself.

Finding yourself struggling to push through a crowd suggests there is a conflict between your conscious and subconscious desires; you are inhibiting the natural flow of your wishes.

902 dirt

To dream of being covered with dirt warns of a loss of favor with important people; your adversaries may be waiting for you to make a wrong move.

903 sewer

Dreaming of being in a sewer suggests the need to reinstate your reputation by ridding yourself of an offensive or antisocial habit.

904 dreaming of being awake

To dream that you have woken up only to find later that you are still dreaming means you must wake up to a challenge or responsibility that cannot be ignored any longer.

905 dizziness

Dizziness or clumsiness in a dream is a call for simplification and discipline in your waking life.

906 shame

Dreams involving shame are related to your self-image and possibly your relationship with your parents; try not to be so self-critical.

907 humiliation

Dreaming of being humiliated may indicate your need to examine the way in which you demonstrate pleasure or satisfaction from recent achievements.

908 shrinking

Shrinking in a dream may touch on your inability to escape from a commitment that you are only halfheartedly performing.

909 growing bigger

Dreaming about growing bigger suggests that you feel destined for better things while a mundane task is dominating your attention. Remember that small steps lead to great achievements.

910 rejection

Dreaming of rejection corresponds to troubling feelings of unworthiness in your waking life, but it may also refer to your own need to distance yourself from an unwanted influence.

911 betrayal

To dream of betrayal indicates that your loyalty or that of a close friend will be tested in the near future; the outcome will be positive if you are prepared to enter a new level of trust.

912 slow motion

Moving in slow motion represents your inability to keep up with the pace that someone else has set; proceed at your own speed.

913 silent scream

Trying to scream but making no sound is a common dream experience; it is linked to a difficulty in your waking life that causes frustration and fear whenever you attempt to verbalize your deep concerns.

914 body part

To dream of growing a body part, such as an arm, leg, or tail, indicates confusion surrounding a physical relationship; do not expose yourself to unnecessary risks.

915 paralysis

Paralysis in a dream puts you into the position of observer; you should pay heed to something that you have ignored because of your alacrity and desire to please.

losing hair

When your hair falls out in a dream, you may be blaming feelings of stagnation on what you perceive to be a decline in mental or physical faculties; do not let natural aging diminish your love of life.

917 unable to see

To dream of being unable to see clearly or to open your eyes fully indicates that you are ignoring a painful truth; face your fears and they will diminish.

918 unpleasant odor

Smelling an unpleasant odor in your dream reveals that there is something distasteful in your emotional life; if, in the dream, others notice the smell, it may mean that your actions are harming loved ones.

919 losing teeth

When, in a dream, your teeth become loose or fall out, you may lack confidence about something that is troubling you and making you feel like a failure.

920 rapid aging

If you age rapidly in your dream, it expresses your perceived loss of control over a matter that may affect your future happiness or financial security.

921 infectious disease

If you feel threatened by an infectious disease, things may be falling apart around you; you will be required to adapt yourself to the demands of a delicate situation.

922 loud noises

Uncomfortably loud noises in a dream correspond to the strongly held misconceptions and delusions of others that you lack the power and influence to overcome.

923 body odor

If you suffer from unpleasant body odor in a dream, it indicates that you will have a serious disagreement with a friend or possible separation from a loved one.

924 dandruff

If dandruff features in your dream, it reveals that your accomplishments threaten to isolate you from others, leading to mistrust and misunderstanding.

925 bad breath

If you suffer from bad breath in your dream, it corresponds to feelings of guilt about something you have said that might have caused distress and hurt.

926 breaking a bone

To break a bone in your dream is a warning that a misunderstanding will cause worry and hardship concerning your health or your finances.

In a dream, falling without injury denotes an unfounded fear of failure. If you incur an injury, you are harboring guilt that is affecting your self-esteem.

928 breaking limbs

Breaking any of your limbs in a dream hints at mismanagement and hasty planning. Is there something you have overlooked?

929 warts

If you are covered in warts or sores in a dream, you will be unsuccessful in defending an attack on your reputation.

930 ambulance

In a dream, an ambulance may symbolize fear of failure and of having to relinquish responsibility to a third party after an error or accident.

931 hurting someone

Hurting someone in your dream indicates that you should consider the effect that your behavior is having on those around you.

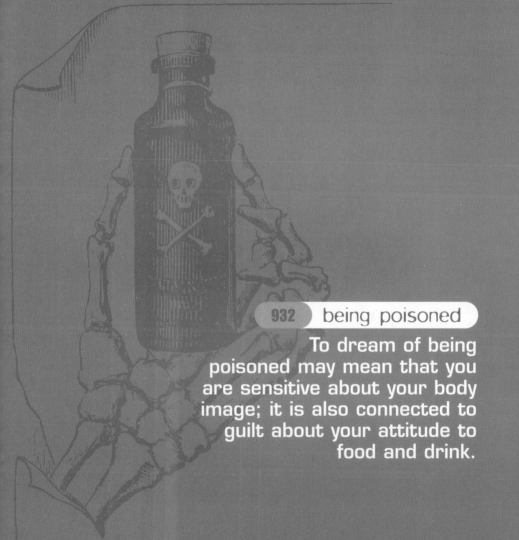

932 being poisoned

To dream of being poisoned may mean that you are sensitive about your body image; it is also connected to guilt about your attitude to food and drink.

933 operation

To dream of being conscious during an operation indicates that others may be making decisions that will affect you directly without consulting you.

934 injection

Dreaming of undergoing a painful injection may refer to having something foisted on you that should not be your responsibility.

935 autopsy

To witness or perform an autopsy in a dream indicates bad management of your affairs; do not be tempted to resort to dishonest means in order to advance your schemes.

936 amputation

To dream of amputation means that you will experience significant loss in business or a time of upheaval and considerable change.

937   being scolded

To be scolded or burned in a dream means that you will experience ill health and quarrels; it may also indicate a dispute to be settled by legal proceedings.

938   scars

Discovering scars on your face or body indicates a need to make something known before half-truths become public knowledge and damage your reputation.

gain or lose weight

To gain or lose excessive weight during a dream touches on your need to protect yourself from a painful memory that is giving you a negative body image.

940 being sick

Being sick in a dream is an expression of possible ambivalence toward something pleasurable that also contains intrinsic physical risks.

941 emergency

If you are faced with an emergency in your dream to which you are unable to respond, it may indicate that you have been troubling yourself unnecessarily about the outcome of recent actions.

942 terminal illness

To suffer from a terminal illness in a dream is a warning of the breakdown of relationships through complacency and insensitivity; it also relates to envy or the bearing of a grudge.

A scythe isn't necessarily a symbol of death; in a dream it can be viewed as the sign of a new beginning and of the completion of a task so that you may move on to a fresh challenge.

944 harm

When a person wishes to harm you in a dream, he or she often represents an aspect of your own personality that is detrimental to your well-being and is making you feel powerless.

945 tied up

If you are tied up in your dream, it means that you are going through a time of diminished influence, but it may also signify the power of passive resistance.

946 sharp objects

Sharp objects that become a threat may refer to the pinnacle of success and the realization that decline must swiftly follow.

947 fight

If you are involved in a fight in a dream, it may mean that you will have an unpleasant confrontation in business; seeing others fighting may be a warning that you are wasting your resources.

948 imprisonment

Being imprisoned is a warning of misfortune unless you acknowledge your strengths and focus on the needs of those around you.

If gallows feature in your dream,
it is likely that an indiscretion
is weighing on your mind.

When a friend fails to recognize you in a dream, it signifies feelings of guilt and unworthiness about what you perceive to be your true nature.

951 blindfolded

Being blindfolded in a dream means you will be called upon to settle a disagreement that will require you to be impartial and objective.

952 power outage

A power outage in a dream denotes financial risk and the need to proceed with extreme caution; you may face a period of volatility and disquiet.

953 guillotine

To dream of a guillotine means that you will have a narrow escape from injury or the designs of enemies; do not lose your head if your path takes an unexpected turn.

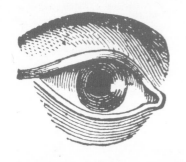

954   evil eye

Dreaming of the evil eye suggests a mistrust of those with an unusual appearance.

955   wild person

A wild person in your dream symbolizes an aspect of your own personality that you dislike and wish to change; if you are attacked or chased, self-deception is harming your prosperity.

A dream about clowns and
the masks that they wear is
frightening for many and one
that calls for more honesty.

957 unknown threats

If you dream of unknown threats lurking
just out of your range of vision, your
subconscious is warning you to be
watchful for dimly perceived hazards
and disregarded drawbacks.

958 being chased

To dream that you are being chased suggests that you feel overwhelmed by an important occasion or meeting and that you feel secretly unworthy of your position or unsure about the value of your contribution.

959 being watched

Dreaming that you are being watched expresses an unconscious desire to be noticed, especially if you have been working quietly and unobtrusively with little reward or recognition.

960 being arrested

Dreaming that the police are trying to arrest you for something you didn't do suggests that although there may have been a misunderstanding in your life, those around you will soon realize your motives are sound.

961 being kidnapped

Being kidnapped in a dream represents a fall in fortunes and a downturn in financial circumstances; attempting to mitigate any losses will bring you into conflict with a trusted friend.

pickpockets

If someone picks your pockets in a dream, it may touch on your reluctance to disclose an idea to others in case they take the credit.

963 being robbed

To be robbed in a dream may relate to the use of strong-arm tactics by a business colleague in relation to your career development; avoid danger by accepting the advice of a respected mentor.

In a dream, being swallowed by a large animal such as a whale may correspond to a feeling of being controlled by a dominant partner, parent, or boss. Your own need for security may be causing your inaction.

965 monster

In a dream, a monster may correspond to anger expressed toward you by someone in your waking life. Children are especially prone to this kind of dream.

966 being bitten

Being bitten in a dream is a sign of deep anxiety about being overwhelmed by unconscious animal forces and repressed memories.

If wild animals surround you or your house, it suggests that you are especially tuned in to feelings of envy from your neighbors or close family; do not make light of your achievements simply to ward off any bad feeling.

968 doppelganger

If you see your alter ego in your dream, your need for objectivity in a situation is affecting you personally; composure now will prevent you from reacting disproportionately later.

969 aliens

Dreaming of aliens expresses your fears of the unknown, especially strangers.

970 transforming into an animal

If you dream of transforming into an animal and find this disturbing, it may indicate that you have been trying to contain your feelings instead of allowing yourself to express some powerful emotions.

971 turning into a werewolf

Turning into a werewolf indicates a desire to appear unconventional in order to raise your standing within a group in which you feel subdued and uncomfortable.

972 giants

A dream about giants alludes to feelings of inferiority or immaturity and is often related to wealth; try not to base your self-esteem on the size of your bank balance.

973 leeches

A dream involving leeches relates to the unwanted attentions of false friends; be alert for those who wish to exploit your generosity or hospitality.

974 spiders

If you dream of spiders, you should be diligent and energetic in any shared undertaking; if mistrust creeps into your enterprises, it will take much work to restore mutual faith.

Cockroaches imply that you will be beset with numerous problems that will undermine your reputation and may cause untrustworthy people to turn against you.

976 infestation

To dream of an infestation suggests the need to take vigorous action to prevent the mismanagement of excessive wealth.

Dreaming of a swarm of insects expresses your sense of bewilderment at being overwhelmed by arguments or unexpected changes in your waking life; it expresses your feelings of powerlessness and loss of control.

978 avalanche

Dreaming of being caught in an avalanche suggests that you are troubled by a problem that you feel will inevitably cause you harm; it also implies repeated danger.

979 hurricane

If a hurricane appears in your dream it indicates that circumstances are moving too fast for you to keep track; try not to feel panicked.

980 earthquake

An earthquake in a dream may be connected with an embarrassing situation that you were unable to avoid because someone changed the rules or altered a routine on short notice.

981 disaster

Dreaming of failing to stop an impending disaster is often a sign that you are expecting too much of yourself and are trying too hard to control your immediate environment.

982 end of the world

To dream of the end of the world suggests anxiety about being judged and fear of the consequences of possible social isolation.

983 temperature

Uncomfortable extremes of temperature in a dream foretell unexpected delays in the accomplishment of plans because of unfavorable external conditions.

984 fire

Usually fire represents
transformation and
purification, but in a
nightmare it stands for
your resistance
to change.

985 flood

To dream of a flood means that powerful emotions threaten to overwhelm you; hesitating to accept your position will lead to unfortunate ventures.

986 war

Dreaming of war indicates anxiety about factors that you feel are out of your control; those in a position of power may seek to trick you into taking hasty action.

987 tornado

A tornado in your dream relates to transformation through a powerful experience; remain committed when facing a demanding challenge.

988 tidal wave

A tidal wave represents a powerful emotional need that is dominating your daily life and possibly damaging your interaction with others.

989 contamination

To dream of chemical contamination indicates that there is a corrosive or caustic influence in your waking life; failure to take action now will have significant and damaging repercussions.

990 deceased

Dreaming of someone who is deceased may mean you need to face up to unfinished business or accept advice from an instinctive area of your psyche. It may also herald rebirth and fresh insights.

991 being strangled

To dream of being strangled indicates that a close friend is harboring hurt feelings; you feel unable to swallow your pride and offer an apology.

992 vampire

To dream of a vampire may refer to a situation in which you will exploit your role as a victim in order to gain the upper hand.

993 suffocating

To dream of suffocating denotes discomfort within a romantic relationship that is smothering your creativity and draining your energy.

994 quicksand

Sinking in quicksand suggests an unconscious awareness of deceit with respect to an agreement; read the small print and be wary of enticements.

995 drowning

To dream of drowning often refers to a social situation in which you feel inadequate in terms of etiquette and decorum; you should also examine what is dragging you down in your waking life.

A shipwreck denotes failure in business; if you swim to safety, then your expertise will be called upon during a financial crisis.

To dream of attending your own funeral speaks of your need for confirmation from loved ones that you continue to hold an important place in their lives.

998 death of a loved one

When a loved one dies in a dream, it may
express your unconscious desire to spend less
time with that person and strike out on your
own. Acknowledge feelings of guilt and move on.

999 buried alive

Dreaming of being buried alive
reflects waking concerns about
mortality and illness.

1000 heaven and hell

To dream of heaven and hell expresses
your search for spiritual or emotional
truth; they are inevitably linked to
feelings of guilt and unworthiness and
the desire to examine your conscience.

First edition for North America published in 2004 by
Barron's Educational Series, Inc.

First published by MQ Publications Limited
12 The Ivories
6–8 Northampton Street
London, N1 2HY
email: mqpublications.com
web site: www.mqpublications.com

All inquiries should be addressed to:
Barron's Educational Series, Inc.
250 Wireless Boulevard
Hauppauge, New York 11788
http://www.barronseduc.com

International Standard Book No.: 0-7641-2723-3
Library of Congress Catalog Card No.: 2003108150

Editor: Karen Ball
Design concept: Balley Design Associates
Design: Philippa Jarvis

Printed and bound in China
9 8 7 6 5 4 3 2 1